The 41 L
Learn
Vol. 1

"41 indisputable, ironclad business truths that will eradicate your frustration, overwhelm and self-imposed entrepreneurial slavery"

Written & Narrated By:

Troy A. Broussard

The 41 Laws
of the Learniverse
Vol. 1

Written & Narrated By
Troy A. Broussard

Published by TroyBroussard.com LLC
13506 Summerport Village Parkway
Suite #714
Windermere, Florida 34786
www.troybroussard.com

For more information, please read the "Disclosures and Disclaimers" section of this book.

TABLE OF CONTENTS

INTRODUCTION

"The First Meaning of the Title"

So what the heck is the Learniverse anyway? Seems like a very odd title. Well trust me, there is a method to my madness. In fact, the Learniverse has two different contexts that I'm referring to.

In the more general sense, I am referring to the world of entrepreneurial learning based content — digital courses, training programs, audio books, digital PDFs, articles and more. Online learning has become a massive space in the past few years, one I refer to generically as "the Learniverse".

For the purpose of this book, I'm generally excluding traditional schools and formal education and referring more to the universe of entrepreneurs, the movement of the new educators. More and more business men and women have traded in their corporate jobs and have begun to capitalize on their individual experience and history to become authors, consultants, speakers, trainers, bloggers, podcasters, YouTubers and other forms of social influencers. They have exited the universe, turned right (haha), and found themselves deep in the Learniverse.

Like any universe, there are laws that govern how the it functions. For example, gravity, time, and Newtonian physics govern our universe.

Likewise the Learniverse has its own laws as well. And just like the Law of Gravity, it doesn't really matter whether you believe in them or not, they just are.

Gravity doesn't concern itself with your beliefs. You can challenge it, question it, disbelieve all you want, but when you drop that plate, it will come crashing down and shatter in a 1000 pieces. Laws are immune to belief.

Many entrepreneurs find themselves lost at first, in a new Learniverse without any laws to guide them. And thus was the beginning of this book.

"The Second Meaning of the Title"

The second reason for the reference to the Learniverse in the book title is more personal. It ties back to my mobile learning platform, Learnistic™, and that of my business partners Ben and Stefania Settle.

Learnistic was created to make it easier for online entrepreneurs to create, teach and reach their audiences — where there audiences live — on their mobile phones — without having to be a nuclear engineer to deal with all of the tech nonsense. If you want, go ahead and take it out for a free test drive yourself, no credit card required, at Learnistic.com.

New online entrepreneurs are forced to drink from the firehose of technology in order to try and get their courses created, published and making them money. They have to become wizards at website design, email and marketing automation, a plethora of software for audio and video editing, memberships sites to house their content and shopping carts to sell it. It's insane.

And then, even after they manage to pull that rabbit out of the digital hat, they realize that their distribution channel is archaic — the desktop pc — you're familiar with that ole dinosaur, aren't you?

We live in a mobile society. The average American spends more than 5+ hours a day on their mobile phone, touches it 2,617 times per day and spends 92% of that time inside of a mobile app. Desktop use is dwindling while mobile use continues to grow. These trends are even further exacerbated in third-world countries like Africa where landline infrastructure for Internet connectivity is very poor, or non-existent, but mobile is prolific.

I created Learnistic to make the solo entrepreneur's life easier, simpler and insanely more affordable than developing your own app. But more than cost savings, it's really about freedom and enabling the mobile lifestyle. Notice my choice of words — the *mobile* lifestyle. The laptop lifestyle too is going the way of the desktop. People want simple and their phone is always available, their notebook? Not so much.

Learnistic really has created its own Learniverse as the rules for success online today are shifting but very few are adapting quickly to those shifts. The shift away from email, away from the tethered desktop, even away from the bulky notebook. In fact, even tablet usage has plateaued in comparison to mobile.

The tides have clearly changed and the purpose of Learnistic is to give those online entrepreneurs a new powerful and über affordable weapon in their business arsenal.

This book also is geared towards my Learnistic clients, but don't worry you won't find but a trifle few references to it throughout the book. I really hate thinly veiled advertising masquerading as an educational book. You know the type, those cheesy sales pitch oriented books designed to pimp out a product or service providing little or no value. This is not one of those books.

That being said, I won't shy away from the fact that Learnistic is a game changer and it is mentioned in some areas as it does make sense. After all, it is my baby and we all carry a few baby pics on our phones, right?

"Why 41 Short Chapters"

Short, pithy, insightful and entertaining — those are my goals for you with this book. Long chapters are dull to read and honestly this book was written to be listened to as much as it was read.

That in and of itself is a bit of an unveiling of the way I think and how committed I am to mobile first. I created this book to appeal to listeners first, readers second, and listeners enjoy short and direct segments of content that are easily consumed.

Probably the best way of describing it that I can think of is how my dear friend and Learnistic client, Greg Rollett, calls it — "snackable content". By keeping the chapters short, it's easy to bite of a small snack and come back for more later, when it's convenient. For that reason, the audio version of this book has chapters that are just 3 to 7 minutes in length.

"41" though has its own very special significance to me. My grandfather, Edward Lovay Williams, born 9/19/1919, the youngest of 19 children (all true), was very superstitious and had all kinds of beliefs around numbers and whether they were good or bad. The numbers we talked most about were 13, 19 and 41.

My grandfather, Papa as I called him, was a kind and fun man and like a second father to me. He also had a very healthy respect for authors. He looked up to them, and though he never wrote a book, he was quick to mention various authors that he looked up to and respected.

I know he would have loved to have known that I became an author, though he passed away before my first book. So in all of my books, to honor him, I always write either 13, 19 or 41 chapters as a way of paying homage to Papa and somehow, somewhere, causing a little twinkle in his eye.

"About Troy"

I grew up far too fast, and, in many ways, my childhood was cut short when, at 10, my 18-year-old sister, Traci Janine Broussard, was killed in a traffic accident which was the result of a bizarre set of circumstances that all culminated into the perfect storm that somber day in 1980.

Though I miss my sister dearly, I am eternally thankful to her and the profound influence she has had on my entire life. Yes, I grew up too quickly. Yes, I lost some of my childhood. Yes, it was a difficult time for our entire family. But through it all, I learned the power of NOW and living as if there were no tomorrow.

I have lived a very full and blessed life thanks, in large part, to my sister. She gave me the courage to move away from home at just 13 years old and attend a private boarding school. That taste of independence, which came from a desire to attend the school she had once attended, led to an insatiable quest for self-sufficiency, travel and learning that has defined my entire life.

At 16, I traveled to Brasil (native spelling) as an exchange student, and, at 17 with a parental waiver, I enlisted into the Navy's Nuclear Propulsion program onboard submarines. Then later I earned an NROTC scholarship to the Illinois Institute of Technology, and a quick trip down the path of hard knocks, as I dropped out of college and began my own path.

I have been fortunate to have had many careers in my life, from being a software salesman at Egghead (oh, remember those days?), to a self-taught programmer working at Blue Cross Blue Shield and Encyclopædia Britannica, a land developer, a general contractor, a cabinet shop owner, an SEO services provider, a trainer, a coach, an author, a consultant and a SaaS company builder.

I have been very blessed indeed, but I was not lucky. Those are two very different things.

I believe in opening your mind and your own doorways — creating your own luck. My former SEO company — which grew to a multi-million-dollar business inside of 22 months and to a staff of 110 during that same timeframe — was built while I lived overseas, with a terrible Internet connection, in a third-world country, and during the worst economic depression (at that time) since The Great Depression.

You CAN create your own economy!

It is amazing what the universe will conspire to bring to you when you're simply willing to first provide for others without expectation.

I'm an instrument-rated private pilot and an avid family man who loves to travel. I make my homes on the West Coast in Southern Oregon, the East Coast in Florida and in São Paulo, Brasil — frequently traveling between them. I've also lived the nomadic entrepreneurial lifestyle for up to a year at a time, working on the road while traveling full time with the family throughout the country.

At 50, at the time of writing this book, I can tell you I cherish, first and foremost, freedom, and strive to continually improve and refine my four businesses to provide ever more freedom while still growing.

I'm blessed to have a beautiful, loving wife, Edina, who is the love of my life. Ever supporting and uplifting, I've rarely ever seen her upset. Not one of those false-happy people, but, rather, a strong, quietly confident in her own skin, rock of eternal contentment and happiness. She wakes up happy and content each and every day, and is the absolute joy of my life. Together, we have two children, and I have two older children who live near their mom in Brasil and frequently travel to visit with us several times a year.

Passion. Freedom. Family. That about sums me up.

LAW #1

OF THE LEARNIVERSE

"Get In or Get Out"

https://learnistic.com/4101

Much of the world is filled with soft people who are afraid of being themselves. You can position yourself radically different than 90% of your competition by simply staking your claim, holding the line, and creating black and white sets of guidelines and rules which govern your society and culture.

When I say, "govern your society and culture," I mean the culture that you're fostering and creating within your own business. Because, in the end, that's what is going to make you uniquely different from any other alternative and prevent you from ever being copyable.

Others cannot be you and cannot copy your unique approach, style and charisma. The only way to prevent your business from being copyable is lead with unabashed candor.

The concept of black and white guidelines rubs a lot of people the wrong way, because they are incapable of deciding what those guidelines are — and have trouble sticking to them. Their decision-making tends to be in the moment and is influenced by their emotions as opposed to a well-constructed, preemptively decided outcome.

What do I mean by a preemptively decided outcome? This is all about deciding in advance, seeing the outcome before you start into some course of action, knowing it to be true, and not doubting yourself along the way because you have already made that decision.

For example, I read that Sir Richard Branson uses this technique to remain faithful to his wife. As a successful billionaire and business mogul, he has the opportunity to cheat on his wife with much younger women almost daily.

So in order to not be tempted, each day when he kisses his wife goodbye in the morning, as he heads out, he makes a conscious decision that today will not be the day he cheats on his wife. Later, when the opportunity arises, he's firm and resolute because he already made his decision. It was made in advance.

The get in or get out law reduces things down to an easy, simplistic standard that allows you to not get bogged down in the decision-making process in the moment. It really is simple: the events confronting you are either in alignment or out of alignment. There is no other option.

One of the ways I practice this in my business is in my coaching calls. I run a group coaching program for business entrepreneurs. It has a very simple policy: "Show your face or get off the call."

The calls are on Zoom, which is an audio and video-based meeting and webinar platform. I have found many people at the beginning of the coaching program would prefer to sit on the sidelines and not engage by being on the call, but without their video turned on. I don't let them get away with this. In fact, I say "oh *hell* no" to the concept and remove them from the call if they don't come on video.

Why?

Because I want people who are fully engaged and present. I feel it's only fair and respectful to both myself and everyone else also on the call.

If they can't be on video because they're on a phone or don't know how to turn on their camera, I'll help them. But I am concerned about the people who do not turn on their camera because that means they are not fully committed to the meeting.

I'm there fully showing up as a coach, giving my 100% to everybody on that call — so I won't accept anything less from them. If they want to watch the recording later, that's fine, but they're not going to be just watching TV or mindlessly surfing around Facebook while listening in the background. That is just disrespectful of everyone's time and commitment so I'm black and white on this subject.

If you want to be on the live call, be on the call — be present, be attentive and turn your video on. Get in or get out.

I also have a strict "get in or get out" policy related to Learnistic, my mobile customer management and learning platform.

If someone cancels or drops off the subscription, they are not allowed to come back in.

There are many reasons why I have this policy and it's far too in-depth of a subject to cover in a short chapter like this. In fact, it's probably an entire book of its own. But the bottom line is: I want people who are committed. If they decide my platform isn't for them, that's fine — but then they're out and there's no coming back.

Simply put: I won't work with indecisive people. They're the same people who generate a lot of support tickets, like to point fingers at you and everyone else for their lack of commitment, with no self-awareness or personal responsibility. That's something I simply won't accept. I choose not to work with people that love to hold everyone else to a higher standard while simultaneously justifying and rationalizing their own lackluster effort.

I'm a military man. All I ask is that you give it your all, very simple. This may not be easy, but it is quite simple. Insisting on seeing your face on video and not allowing reentry into my platform may seem brash and harsh to you, but they are guidelines that I've made out of compassion and without judgment.

Telling someone "no" can be the best thing you can do for them even though it feels just the opposite. When you say, "No, you can't be on the live coaching calls unless you engage and turn your video on," you're doing them a favor. If they decide to cancel because of that policy, then it shows their lack of desire to do what is needed (big or small, like turning on their camera) to improve their business. And if that's the case, what better thing can you do then to refuse to take money from them and allow them the opportunity to spend that money elsewhere?

I hold people to a higher standard — a standard of *investment*, not waste. I refuse to disrespect their investment by not allowing them to get the most from it. And if that means that I lose them as a customer, then I'm okay with that. There's really nothing more compassionate than preventing people from wasting their own money and time. That's what this "get in or get out" policy does — it protects them from themselves and that, to me, is a very respectful thing to do.

Yes, it's confrontational to say, "No, I won't take your money," but it's tough love and preserves the integrity of your platform, which brings us to the second point:

It's not just about them.

This is your platform — something you've spent years or maybe even decades of your life bringing to fruition. Which is why you must protect it from the non-engaged and non-committed people of this world who will do nothing to help move your platform forward and their very association with it will do nothing but weaken and cripple it.

I choose to only allow people into my platforms who are like-minded and will generate referrals and longtime customers to come. For those who don't go down my path, that's totally fine — there's no judgment on my part. I simply nip it in the bud and cut them off early and free them to pursue their approach with someone else more tolerant of mediocrity.

When I ban someone from ever coming back into my software platform, it's not out of indignation, nor is it judgmental — it's simply letting go of someone who's not an ideal client. See, I don't want a bunch of so-so clients; I want ideal, raving clients. The type of client who wants to go out and create a culture and a movement that grows on its own organically and virally. That can't be created when you have uncommitted, wishy-washy types amongst your ranks. Those must be flushed out and quickly.

Get in or get out.

LAW #2

OF THE LEARNIVERSE

"Lead, Don't Ask!"

https://learnistic.com/4102

It probably comes as no surprise to you that a military man would be all about leadership. I grew up with a very discipline-oriented father. I learned from an early age to either lead, follow, or get out of the way. As an owner of a company, even if you're just a solo entrepreneur, you are the leader of the company. But the question is: are you leading it?

Most people want to follow and that's perfectly fine. But leadership is a requirement if you have a mission you wish to impart upon the world and you formed a business in order to extol those virtues. As Rush sings in *Freewill*, "If you choose not to decide, you still have made a choice." It comes down to personal responsibility.

I'm not here to cast judgment and say which is right and which is wrong, because I don't believe in right and wrong — I believe in what is right for me. That said, there are two basic types of businesses:

1. Pioneers

Also known as trailblazers, they are focused on innovation, leading the way with new ideas and concepts, or products that may not even exist yet. They often display brash confidence, charisma, and strong leadership, daring people to follow.

2. Refiners.

Unlike pioneers, refiners aren't trying to innovate an industry but rather looking to improve an already existing process. By focusing on fine-tuning an industry, they tend to ask a lot of questions of their users to determine their wants and needs, which drives the direction of their company.

Both business types can be successful. But the billion-dollar companies are led by pioneers with strong leadership abilities. Meanwhile, the streets of failure are littered with low six-figure companies that are struggling to get by, beholden to every whim and want of their customer base.

The fundamental flaw with asking your users what they want is that they don't know what they want. They're looking to you as an expert — as somebody who has experience, wisdom and hopefully a unique insight into their business. They are looking to you to provide guidance and often to do the thinking *for* them so they can just simply follow your lead. Even when they may say they know what they want, it might not be what they *need*.

There's the old story about Henry Ford. When it came to abiding by his customers' whims, he said "any customer can have a car painted any color that he wants, so long as it is black."

- In a horse-drawn carriage world, Henry Ford brought us the Model T — even if it only came in black.

- Steve Jobs never asked if people wanted an iPhone. He simply created the most disruptive technology ever released in a mobile platform. His phone was something so simple and elegant that anyone could respect the innovation, even if they weren't Apple fans. His phone defined, and continues to define, an entire era of mobile technology.

- Thomas Edison didn't ask people if they wanted a light bulb. He created the vision of what he intuitively saw for them, preemptively answering their need before they ever realized it existed.

Today, we are in a "me too" society — where a tactic that works short-term is copied blindly, without question, by everyone. As business owners, we're told that "the customer is always right" and to cater to their every whim. This creates a business based on pandering to the lowest common denominator.

See, those who ask — for more options, different features, or, as in Henry Ford's case, new colors — are those who complain, and it's a well-known fact that complainers are far more outspoken than the comfortable, complacent, satisfied customers who are too busy enjoying their product to give you their feedback. So when you design a company built around asking people what they think they want, you're really catering to the lowest common denominator — the lowest quality of customer who will cause you endless support tickets, grief, high churn rates, and low referral rates.

Why? Because you listened to what they said they wanted and gave them what they *thought* they needed.

Now, there are many systems that teach you to build your business by asking and serving people and crafting your offers and your products and services around what they say they want. I'm not judging this as the wrong way of doing things — it is simply not the way I do things for all the reasons I've stated above. It comes down to a choice that, as the leader of your company, you must make:

You can either choose to set yourself apart, innovate, and pioneer a path, blazing a trail that people will follow you down. Or, you can refine the processes of others and give people what they think they want and deal with the mediocrity it creates.

Let's take a final military word on the matter, do you think an officer ever asks his troops to charge the hill or does he simply command them to do so and lead by example as the first one in the line?

A lot of people tend to think commanding officers stand in the back and put their soldiers in harm's way. And, in some cases, that's true. But revolutionary leaders in the military are always those who lead by example.

When I was going through the Navy Reserve Officer Training Corps program, the base executive officer (XO) was a Marine Corps colonel. He was a brash, semi-deaf, harsh leader who led by example in every exercise we undertook, including the simple act of entering the "chow line" where he refused to eat until each soldier ate first. He put them ahead of himself at every step of the way. Even into his fifties, he led the pack when we were running drills. He didn't observe from afar — he led from in front. And he certainly didn't ask if you wanted to get up at 0500 hours or commence PT at 0530.

No. For me, the choice is simple:

Lead, don't ask.

LAW #3

"The Dichotomy Dogma Demolishes the Delusionally Dull"

https://learnistic.com/4103

We all have two versions of ourselves, two separate inner voices, that often are in direct contradiction to one another. One tries to protect us and the other urges us forward. I like to call them "the wimp" and "the badass."

The dichotomy of these two opposing forces is a struggle that every one of us faces. However, the difference between your regular, ordinary accountant and, say, a UFC (ultimate fighting championship) fighter is which voice they ultimately listen to.

Most people in society — about 95% — will listen to and heed that dull voice of reason. While they avoid difficult decisions, they sacrifice huge potential gain for short term comfort. Now, don't get me wrong, for most, this is the right way to go. For a UFC fighter, however, they would never step into the ring if they listened to their inner wimp. No, they summon the badass — that inner Tony Soprano beast that ignites them.

A perfect example of one of those 95% thinkers is Ronald Wayne. Now, if you don't know who he is, that's with good reason. Ronald once owned 10% of Apple, having co-founded it with Steve Wozniak and Steve Jobs in the very early days of the company. But Wayne was not a risk-taker — and ended up giving up billion-dollar fortune, *willingly.*

Here's what happened.

In the very inception of Apple — when they weren't even at the building-computers-in-their-garage stage yet — Steve Wozniak and Steve Jobs decided to partner with Ronald Wayne, carving out a 10% ownership deal for him, with themselves each owning 45% of the company.

But, after joining Apple, Ronald found out that it was a general partnership and not a corporation — meaning, his personal assets could be at risk if the company ever faced any litigation. Shaken by his fear of being personally liable if something potentially went wrong, Ronald sold back his 10% stake for a mere $800 and an additional $1,500 payout later on. What he sold off for $2,300 in total would today be worth about $100 billion. Had he not been afraid, he would have been a multi-billionaire.

When the author Walter Isaacson interviewed him for his best-selling biography on Steve Jobs, Ronald had retired to a mobile home park in Nevada, spending his days gambling on penny slots with almost nothing to his name. That is what listening to his inner wimp instead of fearlessly embracing his inner badass got him, a trailer park lifestyle instead of a yacht.

Being an entrepreneur is a different lifestyle, there's no doubt about it. As entrepreneurs, we don't have the perceived stability of a job — if we don't create income, we don't pay the bills. I like to think of the entrepreneurs of today as modern-day business gladiators. Everything is on the line, all the time.

Notice that I said "perceived stability" above. That is because I know all too well that a job does not guarantee any stability whatsoever. You're always 30 days away from looking for a new job — a fact I learned in 2002 when I was deceitfully fired from a major corporation. There is this false belief that having a job equates to stability, but that pipe dream hasn't been true since the 1950's era of pension plans (if indeed it ever was). Today there are only two constants — change and instability. You likely will change jobs many times in your career, regardless of whether you are an entrepreneur or not.

The entrepreneurial lifestyle forces us into a fight-or-flight mode of operation — one that can serve us well if we learn to embrace that inner dichotomy. There can be a time for being conservative, especially with your money. But, when it comes to decision-making, you need to be aggressive and let that inner excitement, passion, and confidence come out in full color.

As a business owner and entrepreneur, you are a leader — whether you acknowledge that or not — it's the law of business. Just like the law of gravity, you do not have to believe in gravity for the plate to shatter when it hits the ground. The law of gravity doesn't give two cents whether you believe in it or not. Likewise the laws of business impose their will upon you. Be a leader or be content with what you get. It's that simple.

But, here's the thing about leaders, they're nothing without followers. To be an effective leader you need to charismatically inspire people to follow you. You can't do that if you have the personality of a toad. You must call upon that "inner badass" version of yourself to amp up the passion and confidence and put the best version of yourself forward.

I am not saying that you should lie or that you should misrepresent the facts. What I am saying is, you should allow your best energy, passion, leadership and confidence to shine through in what you create. People want to be inspired and they want to follow, but they need to be *led* in order to follow. They don't follow boring, bland, uninspired people — they follow leaders.

Step into your inner badass.

LAW #4

"Relatability Trumps Clever Creativity"

https://learnistic.com/4104

One of the most successful speakers of our time was Zig Ziglar. He was one of the most down-to-earth, relatable people you could ever meet, which was a critical ingredient to his success. He was able to connect with anybody because of his down- home nature. His relatability was his single strongest selling proposition, with his likability a close second.

Today, however, entrepreneurs are encouraged to be clever and creative, and focus on all kinds of marketing using whizzbang, flashy tech, and all sorts of tactical, temporary, and fleeting solutions instead of just focusing on relatability and likability to those they seek to inspire and sell to.

Yes, I did say "sell to." If you haven't gotten over the fear of selling, then you should do all of us a favor and get out of business now — you're really wasting your time and negatively impacting those around you, especially your family and loved ones, by trying to do something that will never be successful until you change your mindset around sales.

Sales is something that any businessperson should love. If they don't, they should learn to develop a love for it and do it in a way that *makes* them love it. Every company is fundamentally in business in order to be profitable. And to do that takes sales and salesmanship.

The two assets you should most focus on are your relatability and likability to your audience if you wish to influence them to buy from you. Zig Ziglar perfected these attributes throughout his career. He was easily the most influential and admired salesman of his time, perhaps ever. He inspired people, he uplifted them, and he always came from a position of positivity and support. And that all came from his relatability and the fact that people just liked him and liked being around him.

People who struggle the most with being relatable are tech specialists like myself. Technologists tend to get overly wrapped up in the tech and lose sight of the human connection that our technology must provide in order to be successful to begin with — because technology for the sake of technology is useless.

The only way technology can empower businesses is through its impact in human connection. Many great businesses formed by technologists have failed miserably, even when their technology was great, because their leadership couldn't understand they needed to be relatable and likable first and foremost. It isn't just about the tech — it's about the likability and relatability of its leadership.

Why? Because people buy from those they know, like, and trust. This is why I'm focused on relatability in this law. It sounds like an obtuse concept, but it's simple — so simple, it's a lesson we learned since we were five years old on the playground:

The kids you liked were the ones who you could just walk up to and play with and hang out with, and not have any fear of approaching. The big, overpowering, imposing bullies of the playground were not. And the know-it-alls who kept you at arm's distance didn't inspire you to want to spend any time with them either.

One of the best books ever written on the subject is *How to Win Friends and Influence People* by Dale Carnegie. It's an all-time classic for a reason — personable relatability always trumps clever creativity.

LAW #5

"Bring Buyers First, The Leads Will Follow"

https://learnistic.com/4105

Why is it that so many online entrepreneurs ignore the way business has been done for centuries?

Imagine a vegetable farmer in ancient Rome handing out free vegetable samples in exchange for a prospect's time — and not having a single fresh vegetable to sell them.

Or worse yet, can you imagine the same vegetable farmer just handing out scrolls with information to passersby about how great his vegetables are, but with none in stock?

These are ridiculous scenarios, I know. But ask yourself: How many online marketers do exactly that? Online business owners have been told to focus on building their lists by giving away free information and "value" before they ever try to make a sale. Oh yes, I'm talking about the "value builders."

Here's a novel concept...

Why not build value in *what you sell* instead? Why not build value through selling something worthwhile, so you help your customer and put a little coin in the bank account too?

Business is refreshingly simple. Don't, however, confuse simplicity with being easy. I didn't say it was easy, I said it's *simple*. People exchange money for things they want or need.

But if all you're doing is providing free information *about* their wants or needs, and not actually fulfilling those needs, you're not doing them any favors and may be irritating them more than your value-building wannabe guru's philosophy promised.

Worse yet, you're likely to run out of money by using this tactic because, while you're building your list hoping to strike it rich later, you're not generating revenue. You're also likely to find out the people on your list — attracted by the so-called "value" you've been building — are not at all interested in the product you ultimately decide to create. Or even if they are casually interested, they're not willing to pay for it.

This is one reason why many entrepreneurs in the last three to five years have turned away from traditional information marketing towards more direct-to-consumer e-commerce endeavors instead. In e-commerce, you know what products are selling and where you should expand as well as what is not selling and should be removed or discontinued from your stock. E-commerce is focused on sales first and filling a need —not trying to build value and trust through information in hopes of making a buck later.

This is not a plug for e-commerce or me saying that e-commerce is an easy route either. I don't operated any e-commerce businesses, though I've consulted on many. But e-commerce is a transactional and sales-oriented style of business. And, unfortunately, if you don't know the niche you're selling in very well, or how to target your ideal buyer, you're not likely to have much success there either.

The easiest approach to take is to try several low-priced offers that target specific pain points in your industry and build a small but rabid list of paying customers —instead of a list of so-called "interested leads" (or what I like to call, "worthless tire kickers"). Running some organic or paid traffic to these low-priced direct offers will quickly verify if you have something people are willing to buy.

Once you've found one that is working well, you can then focus on building out a funnel. But remember, keep it simple. Start with a simple two-product funnel — your low-priced offer and an upsell to your core offer. I know many clients and colleagues who have multi-million dollar businesses doing nothing more complex than that. If it works well for them, why does the typical entrepreneur making only $50k or $60k a year think they need an advanced funnel?

Remember, there's one interesting fact about buyers...

Buyers *buy.*

Yes, I'm saying that tongue in cheek, but it's true. If you focus on building a small but rabid buyers' list, they will be much more likely to buy your next offer as well.

I'd take a list of 1,000 buyers over a 10,000-person list of worthless tire kickers any day. Keeping a relentless focus on getting sales (and not just "interested leads") will make your business into a much more successful and *profitable* one, and ensure you're still in business in the years to come. It will also provide you with the cashflow to expand your list building activities later on. And, with that new larger list you're going to build, you'll know exactly what to sell them because you already have a proven offer!

Buyers buy. That sounds like a pretty powerful segment worth focusing on to me.

LAW #6

"An Offer a Day
Keeps Bankruptcy Away"

https://learnistic.com/4106

One common trait that starving entrepreneurs share is their innate ability to overcomplicate almost anything. It amazes me how many businessmen and women will spend countless hours and even tens of thousands of dollars on crazy complicated funnels and paid traffic campaigns, yet they still haven't overcome the biggest limitation in their business:

The fear of asking for a sale.

This fear is so strong, I'm willing to bet that 90% of users of marketing automation software bought it for the sole reason that they were afraid to ask for a sale and were hoping the software automation could just sell for them on "auto pilot". Unfortunately, I've seen this firsthand with dozens of clients who've sunk tens of thousands of dollars into funnels. And, even if they do manage to generate leads, they don't even follow up with them afterwards because they didn't strike instant riches the first time around. This "income on auto pilot" mantra preached by marketing gurus of today is our modern-day snake oil.

This might seem ironic coming from someone who has been considered one of the go-to guys in marketing automation and funnels. However, the truth is that most people really don't need it. What most business owners need to do is simply engage their audiences more frequently — via email, audio, or video content — and make more offers. There's nothing inherently wrong with marketing automation, when used properly, but technology is not the panacea for a bad offer or a poor business strategy.

Most entrepreneurs would be far better served by keeping technology super simple and focusing on getting one core offer converting well, building their audience, keeping their audience engaged with frequent content, and building revenue (and dare I say, reserves) before investing in complex and sophisticated marketing funnels.

But today's marketing gurus leading the trends — and the sheep who follow them — would have you believe that you're a fool if you don't have a super complex 43-step funnel with six upsells. In my years of coaching, I have seen this same scenario repeated dozens of times: clients spending months or even years building out a super complex funnel before they know if anyone is willing to buy their core product.

Also remember the only vote that counts as to whether you have a good offer or not is the vote that comes from MasterCard, Visa, Amex, PayPal or Discover. Don't rely on friends and family or even colleagues to tell you that you've got a great offer — the only way you truly know is when people vote with their pocketbooks. That's all that counts.

So instead of focusing on complexity, do the opposite and keep your initial product funnel super simple. Focus on consistently making more offers to sell it. Find out what pain points work and what emotional triggers convert. Find out what doesn't work.

How do you do that? Simple. Write more emails and put a call to action in everyone. Release more videos, audios, e-books and other media and in each one of them place a call to action to sell your product.

This is a very simple formula to follow: The more offers you make, the more money you'll make.

Don't buy into the often-quoted myth that you need to "build value" before you sell. Instead, do both *simultaneously* — by building value into the content that you release while asking for a sale at the same time.

If you want to predict your income from this year to next, simply count the number of offers you made this year and double it in the year to come and watch what happens. This is very simple math and there is no need to overcomplicate it.

More offers equate to more sales. Make this the one metric you focus on in the next 90 days and watch the impact on your bottom line.

LAW #7

"Repulsion Crushes the Flaw of Attraction"

https://learnistic.com/4107

There's a lot of talk about the Law of Attraction — but very little mention about its distant often forgotten and frequently dismissed cousin, the Law of Repulsion, a much more powerful alternative. It's so much more powerful that I refer to this as the Flaw of Attraction, because concentrating on it, while ignoring the Law of Repulsion is a critical business flaw.

There's a unique phenomenon that occurs when you focus on *repelling* the people you don't want — you actually end up attracting those you *do* want, and at a much higher rate.

Let me explain:

Imagine you're a woman targeting other women for a female entrepreneurial coaching group. You followed all the advice of the gurus out there who tell you to "attract everybody you can" and "make offers that cast a wide net." So, you craft a sales letter and an offer that is generic and careful not to offend anyone. And, as it turns out, your results are equally generic.

Now, reimagine this scenario: instead of trying to cast a wide net, you instead employ the Law of Repulsion, curating your copy so that it is *indubitably obvious to the most casual observer* that men are not your target audience. You go out of your way to explicitly state that it's an all-female group and use copy that not only specifically makes women feel at home, it drives men to click away, and fast!

With this approach, women resonate with your message, knowing that, by signing up for your offer, they have a place where they can feel at home and not worry about having to dodge lame male sports analogies constantly being thrown their way. In other words, it both simultaneously repels men and magnifies the attraction for women.

The Law of Repulsion operates by uniting people against a common enemy. I'm not saying you should aggressively pick fights or go up against a literal enemy. But by carefully repelling those you don't want, you're creating a much more compelling space for those you do. They will unite with you and feel a bond and culture that is defined by mutuality — including a mutual dislike or distrust of those you're repelling. This creates an "us versus them" environment that is super effective for creating a highly engaged and united fanbase.

One of the most brilliant corporate leaders of our time, Steve Jobs, used this process unabashedly and with relentless pursuit. There is a famous photo of Steve flipping the birdie to IBM while standing underneath their logo. And Steve was well known for his incessant Microsoft bashing.

Steve knew that uniting his fold against a common adversary would doubly solidify and expand his core base, those that worshipped at the altar of Apple. Even though, to this day, Microsoft has a much larger user base, Apple is more profitable and was the first trillion dollar company in history.

The reason that the Law of Repulsion is so much more effective than the Law of Attraction is that there is absolutely zero neediness involved when you focus on repelling those that you don't want. The Law of Attraction can come across needy, overly politically correct, and afraid to take a stance — it's weak.

There's nothing that kills a sale faster than a salesman whose desperation you can smell like a bad cologne. Confidence, on the other hand, is the superpower of all talented salespeople, which they can wisely wield to close more deals than a Florida ice cream truck in July.

In fact, one could argue that sales is almost entirely about confidence. Look at what the Wolf of Walstreet was able to accomplish through sales. He was selling false hope and lies, but he did so with a brash arrogance that convinced people they should buy even if they didn't like the guy. Confidence trumped all.

By leading with the Law of Repulsion, we are employing the Law of Attraction, but as a reverse side effect. By confidently staking our claim while simultaneously repelling those who we don't want in our midst, we're creating an attractive proposition through the confidence that it conveys to those we wish to attract and the exclusion of those they don't want to be affiliated with. We're leading with confidence and that inspires trust and action.

It doesn't mean that you should be rude or attack any group of individuals. If that's the conclusion you're drawing then you're not paying attention. Nor am I saying you have to write repulsive copy to repell — repulsion does not equate to repulsive. I'm simply saying, if you make it very clear who your offer is *not for* and the type of people you do *not want* in the group and emphasize that, you will better attract and curate those you *do want*.

Remember, people watch fictional comic book movies not for the superhero, but for the villain. We know who Superman is, and what his traits and habits are. There's really nothing surprising about Superman. He's so consistent, he's almost boring, and we've known him for years.

However, each new movie introduces a new and more powerful villain who makes us question, "How is Superman ever going to conquer over evil *now?*" It's that obsession with the villain, the unpredictability he/she brings, and the unknown morbid curiosity of what will happen that draws the crowds to the movie, not our interest in the latest iteration of Superman's suit.

When writing repulsion-based copy, spend about two-thirds of your copy repelling those you do *not want* to take you up on your offer, and only about a third of your copy devoted to attracting those who you *do want*. Like anything, there's no hard and fast rule, and you'll need to experiment with it. But the two-thirds ratio is a good starting point as you make this paradigm shift towards repulsion instead of attraction.

At first, this style of writing will likely feel uncomfortable for you. But your comfort level will increase as the zeros in your bank account do as well.

Swim upstream against the trends that everyone else preaches and ignore the Flaw of Attraction. Trade it in for its little-known but much more powerful supervillain, the Law of Repulsion, and watch your universe grow.

LAW #8

"Meticulous Master Baiters Always Come In First"

https://learnistic.com/4108

If you wanted to summarize marketing into a single word that, by grasping it you will get an 80% understanding of the complex process we call marketing, that word would be...

...well there you have it. I just demonstrated the word in action.

I'll give you a hint — it starts with the letter "C".

Those who learn this fine art of meticulously and masterfully baiting their readers into taking the next step, opening that email, reading the content, clicking through to the site — those are the master marketers, the master baiters. It's all about "C" and they know that.

Watching the mastery of an experienced *copybaiter* is like watching a concert pianist execute the perfect glissando. It builds up, one note upon the next, in rapid acceleration. Each step you take leaves you wanting to take the next, to explore, to uncover, to go further, and fast!

And why?

Because you simply don't know what lies around the next turn of the copybaiter's emotional rollercoaster — you just want to get on that ride and see for yourself.

Have you ever watched high-end car commercials on TV? Of course, you have. The advertisers know that the "C-word" dominates, and tease you with it every step of the way. They show off close-ups of its curves, the impeccable detail in the leather interior, punctuated by the sounds of the V-12 motor roaring and then purring. They show the faces of those in astonishment looking at and gloating over the actor as he gets out of the Italian stallion.

You watch in near darkness where you can't quite make out the brand from behind as it explodes, leaping off the road like the badass Italian cat it is...and then...*bam*, the reveal — that quick pan over the Ferrari logo. It passes quickly, then pulls back and momentarily pauses... teasing... tantalizing... then it's over. Masterful marketers know it's all about building up the "C" and amping it up over and over again, however they can.

Yes, if you haven't figured it out by now, the "C-word" is "curiosity." And it didn't kill the cat — it greased the marketers' pockets.

If you learn nothing else about marketing other than to just focus on building curiosity into your copy, you will already be light-years ahead of most businesses. This one principle is so core to everything you do, ignoring it will hasten your peril because, in business, the spoils always go to the master baiters.

LAW #9
OF THE LEARNIVERSE

"Engagement + Consumption Equals Profuse Profitability"

https://learnistic.com/4109

We all like to think our businesses are so different from everything else, so unique. But the reality is, most businesses are driven by a few common axioms — laws that equally dictate the success or failure of that business. This law is one of them.

Engagement plus consumption equals profuse profitability — E+C=P.

It doesn't matter how great your product is — if you can't get anybody to engage with it and consume it, then nothing else matters. You won't get any sales, and even if you do, you certainly won't get any repeat sales. And this is not something that applies uniquely to online marketing.

Think of an old brick and mortar business — say, a plumber's business. In the days when we relied on the yellow pages to find contractors, a plumber had to use different tricks to get engagement which frequently resulted in unique listings in their yellow pages. They would come up with clever slogans, others with cartoon figures — anything to get that engagement and to stand out against the competition. Even in an old school brick and mortar business, engagement matters. They also had clever tricks like naming their company ABC Plumbing Supplies so they'd be the top listing in their category in the yellow pages.

But even a plumber knows that getting you to chuckle at a clever ad or to see their ad first is not enough. They need to get you to call them when you need them. They need you to invite them to your doorstep and allow them to fix your problem so that they can succeed. Engagement alone is not good enough. It takes consumption as well.

Let's look at another metaphor. Look at the public school system. Public school systems are driven by test scores and funding from the government determined upon those test scores. As a result, school districts have resorted to all kinds of tricks in order to get students to consume their content and do well on exams.

One of those tactics is the borderline harassing parents at home if their child has missed multiple days from school. Parents might receive dozens of phone calls from the school principal's office insisting that their child is only a day or two away from not being able to graduate. This is a way of forcing engagement — of forcing consumption. It's certainly the stick and not the carrot, but it's probably more effective for most.

It also happens at an even more basic level. Public schools provide busing services in order to bring your children to school in the first place. They know that if they're not providing an easy way for students to get to school then students will have no chance of engaging and consuming their content and moving forward in the curriculum.

Engagement plus consumption equals profitability. Yes, even the school districts are worried about profitability — because most of their money comes from government funding, they need to prove that that they deserve it and so they use these same tactics I'm teaching here.

When you take this to the online world, this really comes down to getting your content in front of your users, allowing them to easily consume it, and making it interesting and engaging enough so that they come back and want to consume more.

Now, there's lots of different ways that we do this in the online world. But it all starts with the first rule, that even the plumbers and school districts follow:

Go where your clients are.

Today, nearly 70% of all digital content in the world is consumed on a mobile phone. So it's *indubitably obvious to the most casual observer* that you must be on a mobile platform if you want to make engagement and consumption easy for your audience. Go where they are, they're on their phones.

For that very reason my partner Ben Settle and I have invested over a million dollars building our Learnistic™ mobile learning platform.

But technology alone can never solve business problems. Don't fall head over heels into this myth that just making a technology investment is going to solve a business problem. That is a recipe for disaster and, if that is your genuine belief, you'll fail every time.

Technology is like grease for the gears of business. It causes them to spin smoother, to not grind so much, and to last a lot longer. It also causes them to spin *faster*. So, if your business is already spiraling out of control, spending more money on technology will just send it spiraling further out of control, and faster. You first must have a solid business, then add technology to amplify, improve and speed it up.

While owning a mobile learning app is a good first step towards getting a more engaged audience, purchasing a platform and not using it does absolutely *nothing* for you. To maximize engagement on a mobile platform, you'll need to look at new practices for content publication, at potentially more frequent rates of publication, as well as perhaps producing new types of more mobile friendly content in the first place.

But, one thing is certain, the more you can get people to engage with your content, the more likely they are to purchase and consume it. And that is what creates profitability because engagement leads to *fans*, not just customers. Fans will repeatedly buy from you, and be happy to do it. But that only happens if they're getting quality, engaging content from you on a frequent basis.

Boost engagement by distributing your content on a mobile app since studies show they inevitably will always have their phones with them. Keep the content fun, short, valuable and engaging to push more people into your purchases and to decrease the time between their first and second purchases — a key metric for a successful and strong business.

This means that you must focus on these two aspects of both engagement and consumption. To do so, first, get people into your app by giving them a reason to do so.

People are not going to download your app just because they can. You need to give them a reason *why they should* — that is the very first step to boosting their engagement. The biggest mistakes content creators make are not creating *enough* and not doing so *consistently*. Often, content creators will launch a bunch of content at once, but then forget to continue to follow that initial blast with a consistent content publication cycle. Engagement not only requires enough content, it also requires new *fresh* content delivered consistently over time. That consistency is what really builds up their trust.

Think about a podcast. Would you listen to a podcast if it launched with ten great episodes, skipped a month, and then published sporadically without any set schedule? Of course not. The success of a podcast is rooted in both its production of high quality, engaging content and its consistency — listening to it becomes a habit.

Focus on creating short, fun, engaging content and publishing it on a frequent and consistent basis to bring more people into your platform *to regularly consume* your content. Look at it this way, either you're training your clients to engage with you or you're training them to disengage — the choice of how you train them is up to you.

Speaking of consumption, the easiest way to get people to consume and ultimately pay for content inside of a mobile platform is through in-app purchases. Yes, that means you should be using them frequently. In-app purchases provide a near frictionless purchase experience and allow for immediate consumption of your product.

This caters to the binge effect that people have with content. Just like Netflix and Amazon Prime, people love to *binge-consume* their content, so make sure that you give them lots of fresh in-app purchases that they can continually buy from you.

Don't forget to promote your content and in-app offers from your email list as well to drive people to them, have promotions and sales occasionally, in order to encourage that consumption.

Remember, it takes engagement and consumption to produce profitability.

LAW #10
OF THE LEARNIVERSE

"Friction Erodes Sales
Like a California Mudslide"

https://learnistic.com/4110

There's nothing that marketers should avoid more than friction in their sales process. Any marketer or business owner worth their salt knows that they must do everything possible to make it as *easy* as possible for their customers and leads to spend money with them.

The more barriers you put into the purchase process, the less likely you are to make a sale. This is why simple things like one-click upsells and one-click purchase options in Amazon have been so dominant in this industry. Other technologies such as Apple Pay, Google Pay and in-app purchases are based on the same principle — of making it super easy for customers to buy without ever having to grab their wallet in the process. It's all about reducing friction.

This is where mobile platforms and in-app purchases dominate. There's nothing easier than simply tapping a "buy" button, looking at the screen for a Face ID verification, and completing a purchase.

- No need to grab a credit card

- No need to find your wallet

- No need to even have either on hand

You can simply and seamlessly purchase by just verifying who you are, and your app will take care of the rest right through your Google Pay or Apple iTunes account. This is as close to frictionless in the consumer purchase process as you can possibly get. And it is also the strongest reason you should be using a lot of in-app purchases in your app.

Many marketers, however, shy away from using in-app purchases because they're fearful of the 30% fee that Apple and Google charge for the privilege.

That is foolhardy and could be costing your business a lot of money. The intelligent thing to do is use a lot of low-end, super-easy, bingeable in-app purchases within your platform that encourage people to buy and buy frequently. There is nothing you should want to do more in your business than train people to buy, and in-app purchases make that experience seamless and painless.

Don't get hung up over the 30%. You'll more than make up for that with the *volume* of sales you'll make. You're also setting yourself up for more backend sales which are far more profitable anyway. This is where business owners differentiate themselves from marketers.

A marketer obsesses about the 30%, but a business owner knows the backend sales that a low-ticket, easily consumed, front-end offer is going to bring in will more than compensate for that 30%.

It's more than just the sale of the low-ticket offer — the in-app purchasing platform tracks these sales and will maintain this data inside your customer record, so you can gain insight into who exactly purchased these low-end, frictionless, bingeable in-app offers. You then possess the ability to upsell them through your backend processes on more expensive and profitable products and offers. Although in-app purchases can be priced from 99 cents all the way up to $1,000, it's my recommendation that you have the majority of your in-app purchases priced at the $49-and-under price point, with perhaps a few of them up to $199 or $299. When your products are priced above that, you will be giving up a lot of profit to Apple or Google. It would also defeat the purpose of the in-app purchase, which is an instant low-friction no-brainer purchase with a low-dollar price point.

One last point to consider. This type of purchase never requires your customer to physically view or touch their credit card. I know I've said that above, but I am not sure you've fully comprehended the psychological impact of that on the buying process. Many times, just the act of pulling out their credit card from their wallets causes them to pause and reconsider the purchase, "should I really load up this credit card anymore? Maybe I'll wait until next month".

A truly frictionless purchase environment that doesn't even require them to look at their credit card is super powerful.

Look for creative ways to splinter your core product line off into smaller, easy-to-binge in-app purchases that can increase the number of in-app offers you provide inside of your app. This frictionless purchase environment is key to growing your engagement and consumption within your app and driving larger ticket sales on the backend.

Remember, friction repels — so do everything you can to eliminate it and focus on a lot of low ticket in-app purchases. I would recommend having four or five frictionless lead-in products for any large back-end products at a bare minimum, even more is better.

LAW #11

OF THE LEARNIVERSE

"Repel Early,
Repel Often"

https://learnistic.com/4111

It's critical that you set up your business to immediately repel the wrong type of people. There are devastating costs to having the wrong type of people as customers or in your support chain. And these costs are reflected within your business profits as you attend to needy individuals who are not a good fit for your products or services.

First off, you're not doing *them* any favors by taking their money when they're not likely to get success, and you're certainly not doing *yourself* any favors either. You might be tempted to take their money because you need the money. You may want to close the sale even if it means taking on less-than-ideal clients.

I have a 25-plus year history in businesses of all kinds: offline, online, SEO businesses, consulting businesses, training companies, software companies, real estate companies, construction companies, and even cabinet shops. I've created all types of businesses, whether brick and mortar or online-only. And I can tell you that the *single biggest mistake* you can make in business is to take on the wrong customer.

The cost is far worse than not making the sale at all. The problem really comes down to your own personal attitude about money and sales. When you approach it from a position of neediness — afraid to upset a potential lead, or afraid to lose a sale — then all you attract is needy people. And having needy people as a customer base can cause an immeasurable loss of morale for your team and yourself.

Instead, position yourself strongly — and repel the weak, fragile souls who are not likely to be a good fit. Immediately get them out of the fold. I know that it can seem scary at first to focus on repelling customers, especially if you're just starting out in business. And it may seem completely counterintuitive.

When I say to repel them, I don't mean that you should actively try to scare people away. You should simply repel those who are not *your ideal clients* and *only* take on those for which you know you can hit a home run.

This concept of working with ideal clients that are hand selected as opposed to anyone with a heartbeat is foreign to most businesses. And yes, I mean an ideal client, not just a good client. There is a Troyism I like to say, "momentum begets momentum". When you focus on selling to ideal clients it creates a powerful shift in your business because with an ideal client you can create a big transformation and get the big results. Big client results will get you tons of referrals and momentum in your business.

When, however, you choose to focus on just closing "good" clients or "mediocre" clients, well, your results will be moderate at best and hardly lead to any real growth spurts in your business. Worse yet, you will waste a ton of time (likely much more than you would have with an ideal client) and you will have very little to show for it and likely nothing in terms of referrals to come from it.

One type of person you should immediately repel, regardless of who you work with or where you are in your business, is someone who you must talk into a sale. The person you have to convince to buy from you is someone who you should run from as fast as you can. Because if you have to talk them into making a purchase, you'll also have to talk them into:

- showing up for the coaching calls,

- doing their work, and

- making their payments each and every month

This frustrating cycle will only continue until they cancel, ask for a refund, or even file a chargeback after you've already exerted a tremendous amount of time and effort supporting them.

These are the types of people who your copy, messaging and marketing must repel — or else you'll suffer the consequences, consequences which could put you out of business. The key to being the most effective in business is to only work with *ideal clients*.

If you haven't taken the time to define what an ideal client is for you, that's the first step. After you do so, do the contrarian step of listing out all the traits of people you do *not* want to attract (that becomes the more powerful of the two lists by far).

Between those two lists, you'll have a good start at writing a repulsion-based copy and onboarding experience (like we talked about in Law #7) so that you repel the wrong people and attract the right ones who you want to work with.

Remember: repel early and repel often.

LAW #12

OF THE LEARNIVERSE

"Give 'Em the Rope
& Let 'Em Swing"

https://learnistic.com/4112

This may sound like a sadistic way of managing business relationships with customers or employees, but I find it to be very effective. In business, you only have two choices:

You can either choose to trust people, or choose not to — and then put them through an excruciating vetting process.

The thing is, with either choice, there's no guarantee you're going to get any better results. What I found to be the best approach is to instead come from a position of "trust but verify".

My philosophy is to give people the rope with which to hang themselves. I'm very trusting and open, but I'm quick to nip problems in the bud and move on without a second chance or warning.

Giving people the rope to hang themselves is not about setting people up for failure. In fact, quite to the contrary — it's all about setting them up for success and removing the obstacles and impediments that an extensive vetting process would require. It's all about giving them the freedom to excel quickly — and also the constraint that, if they demonstrate any desire to take advantage of that and you, your business, or your services — you sever ties immediately and move on.

An example of this would be someone who emails your help desk before buying and asks about your refund policy. The fact that a person would ask about a refund policy before purchasing from me absolutely guarantees I would not sell to them. The fact they would ask that question means that they're already considering returning my product and, for those reasons alone, I would disqualify from them from buying. I gave them the rope... and they chose to hang themselves with their question and presumption of refundability of my products or services.

Likewise, when it comes to hiring team members, I'm trusting with the hours they claim to be working. However, the first time I catch them misrepresenting their hours will be their last paycheck. No exceptions, no questions, no discussion. They've already demonstrated a fundamental lack of character by taking advantage of my trust, and that is something I do not give second chances for. I don't do it to be judgmental or a jerk. I simply do not wish to surround myself with people of low character, whether they be employees, contractors or customers.

I also find that it's a fulfilling policy to administer as well. It allows you to see and assume the best in people and to trust them for their potential, while also protecting your business by holding them to that level of moral character that you possess. It's rewarding because you don't have to nag, encourage, chastise, shape, and guide people through the process. You simply allow them to be. They choose their own destiny, self-selecting and choosing whether they belong in your fold or not.

Remember, you're designing a business around your own constraints. If you wish to design a business environment where you must devote yourself to your employees, team members, and customers at a level reminiscent of a 14-year-old babysitter, that's your choice. I don't have time for that, nor do I have any tolerance for drama.

People who don't fit into my way of doing business, I simply choose to let go. I wish them well and let them go work with somebody else who wants to be a babysitter. I have far too little time to babysit, so I give them the rope and let 'em swing.

LAW #13

OF THE LEARNIVERSE

"Slay the Elephant Before It Pulverizes You"

https://learnistic.com/4113

This is a lesson I learned a long time ago when presenting from the stage. What I realized quickly is that, as soon as you walk up on stage, people are immediately judging you. From the topic of your presentation, they already have their mind formed about the pink elephant in the room.

Every presentation might have a different pink elephant. It could be:

- Their fear that you're going to deliver a high-pressured pitch.

- The fact that, at this event, everybody seems to be selling $10,000 items, and they're concerned about the price of *your* product.

- Maybe they don't believe you, because they don't believe the grandiose claim on the title slide.

- It may be that the pink elephant in the room is you and your credibility *(or lack thereof)*.

There is always a pink elephant in the room — so your job is to identify it, in whatever product or service you're selling, or even just teaching about from the stage.

Most presenters will, out of fear, hide from the pink elephant. They will often try to avoid the subject. They'll try to carefully articulate and construct their presentations in a way to avoid conflict and avoid the pink elephant that's looming in the background. Their entire presentation, a dance of avoidance.

I am completely different. I purposefully put a slide up in my presentation with a great big pink elephant. No text, no caption — just a white slide with a pink elephant, right at the beginning of my presentation.

This calls out the pink elephant in the room, right from the beginning and draws attention to it. Doing so immediately takes away their fear because, even if you don't slay the pink elephant, you have confronted it and acknowledged it. This builds up credibility with the audience so they can trust you're going to be real with them and not dance around the subject.

Calling out the pink elephant is easily one of the most powerful presentation advice tips I can give you, and it's one few speakers have the confidence to pull off.

Likewise, in anything you do when selling your product, you can and should call out the pink elephant in the room before it stomps on you and pulverizes you like a cockroach. Don't wait for objections. Point them out and disempower them. Take away the sting of the objection before your client basks in it. Point out the reasons why the objection is completely invalid on its face and disarm it.

If nothing else, even if you don't successfully counter the objections, you will certainly earn their trust. That will keep you in the conversation with them in the future, and lead to further engagement. They may still have difficulty believing your explanation or your rationalization of their objection. But, if you call it out, if you acknowledge it, if you bring it to the surface instead of hiding behind it like a coward, you will earn their trust. Everything in this business comes down to trust.

Does your audience trust you?

People do not do business with those they do not trust. And one of the easiest and most consistent ways of earning that trust — without months of effort — is to call out objections in advance. I've used this tactic from stage for the past 15 years. I use it in every business that I own and create, because I know that any business is only as strong as the relationships and the trust created in those relationships.

Do yourself a favor. Quit hiding from the pink elephant and instead call it out, bring attention to it, and boldly confront it, slaying that elephant before it pulverizes you.

LAW #14

OF THE LEARNIVERSE

"The Camera Adds
10 Degrees of Boredom!"

https://learnistic.com/4114

We all know the old saying: "The camera adds 10 pounds." But, there is an even graver truth: going on video will make you seem *more boring*. I'm sorry to say it, but it needs to be acknowledged.

The same is true with audio, but to a lesser extent. Both audio and video are magnifying glasses, but video has a far more powerful lens: it magnifies both your strengths *and* your weaknesses. If you're good and naturally confident on video, that is plainly visible. People can feel, see, and sense it. Your confidence is magnified through the camera.

However, if you're the least bit timid or shy, the camera gives you no slack whatsoever. It will absolutely eat you up and spit you out. You must bring more energy and excitement and create that charisma in your presentation that keeps people's attention. That means you need to add passion, movement, energy, and character — all to amp up your presentations whenever you go on video.

It's all about charisma. Doubt that? Just look at all of the presidential elections in recent history. It is much less about Republican or Democrat and much more about who has charisma and who doesn't. Ronald Regan, Bill Clinton, Barak Obama and Donald Trump — love 'em or hate 'em — they all are charismatic.

Today, people have the attention span of a hyperactive spastic gnat with ADHD. They are not going to keep their attention on your doldrum video. They simply do not have the attention span to do that anymore. Maybe 30 or 40 years ago people could have tolerated duller, more "professional" presentations but, today, people have no tolerance for them whatsoever. And, like I mentioned in the previous Law, within the first three to five seconds, your audience is already judging you, making up their mind about, among other things, whether or not they're going to tune in to the rest of your video or just bail.

That is the cold, harsh truth and reality of being on video.

So, what does that mean? How do you combat that?

You must get into the groove of your inner badass and amp up your energy. Project strength of character. Project your voice, raise your tone, move around more, and act like you believe what you're saying — as opposed to dead-pan reading from a low-energy script as if no one even cared. Because if that's how you present, no one will.

One of the easiest ways to do this on camera is to film standing up. When you're seated, your energy level is naturally very low. But, when you're standing up, you're already moving, more animated, and have to project even more, which naturally gives the appearance of having higher, more palpable energy.

When you see singers performing on stage, they're always standing up. It's rare they sit down, unless they're playing an instrument like a piano. When you're standing up, you are more fluid and display more passion and energy in your video and audio content. Standing up is the first and easiest thing you can do.

Secondly, simply practice a lot. Develop the ability to *objectively* judge yourself. Doing this objectively is a talent in and of itself. You can't come from a needy position of feeding your own ego. Instead, come from a place of painfully clear objectivity that says, "You know what? That was kind of boring. What can I do to make that a little bit livelier?"

One of the things that I like do is to add a little bit of self-deprecating humor. You don't have to be a comedian, but just make fun of something or make light of the situation. If you screw up, rather than editing it out to make it perfect, crack a joke about your screw up and move on. Let your mistake draw people into you, your approachability and your lack of need for perfection. Let them see that you're a human and not a cyborg recording a script.

Let your personality shine through but do it through a magnifying glass. Give your personality a little more strength, depth, loudness, excitement, and definitely a hell of a lot more passion than you "normally" do. And remember, the camera is always going to add at least 10 degrees of boredom.

LAW #15

OF THE LEARNIVERSE

"Entertain or Die"

https://learnistic.com/4115

One of the biggest mistakes that marketers, info product creators, and trainers make today is that they believe the *quality* of their content is what is going to make them successful. But it just doesn't work that way. The *best* product doesn't win out — the best *marketed* product always does, and marketing involves entertainment.

Stop thinking of your content as training and education, and even I dare say infotainment. Instead, go to the extreme — think of your content as *pure entertainment*. Think of it as competing against Netflix or Sunday Night Football.

So, how do you provide not just information but *entertainment*?

The word "infotainment" emphasizes the value of entertainment. You need to focus on that from day one in your content, in order to fully display your personality, and create a fun, exciting environment where people will actually enjoy listening to you.

There are many ways you can accomplish this and honestly, the topic of infotainment is an entire book in and of itself. But here are a few ideas:

- Mix up the environment where you record

- Walk around while you're recording

- Record while you're at the beach or in a different space outside of your usual "work zone"

- Change some aspect of your style and your approach to mix it up

Whether your content is audio, video, or written content, it doesn't matter — the principle is still the same. You need to find a way to make it entertaining, and to make it engaging. It's not a coincidence that more than a few Laws that I've outlined are about engagement — and one of the most important ones is about both engagement *and* consumption. The easiest way to get more engagement and consumption is by being entertaining and fun — and not a dull, boring waste of their time.

Why do people watch stupid cat videos on YouTube? Because they're entertaining — they're easy to consume and it makes them chuckle. What can you do to lighten the mood a little bit? Because let's be very candid here, you're competing with those cat videos for their time and there has to be some payout for them to justify the time.

How can you disarm their objections and distrust? Get them to like you and laugh with you a little bit. And, yes, maybe even get them to laugh *at* you a little bit too, if that's what it takes. Your goal is to be that person at the block party, you know the one, the one tending the grill that is jovial and fun, that everyone enjoys talking to and generally enjoys being around.

I know you might be thinking, "But, Troy, my goal is to educate my audience. I don't really care if they're entertained or not."

Wrong. In fact, dead wrong. Because if you have that mindset your business is dead in the water from day one. It will take a herculean marketing effort in your business to overcome dull and boring and your entertaining competition will make three times as much as you for half the effort.

If your audience is not entertained, they're not going to stick around long enough for you to educate them. So, get over yourself and embrace the reality of the situation.

You first must get them to engage with you, and then you can focus on entertaining them through your education. That is how you get people onboard and keep them. That is how you create an incredible fan base who will buy everything you sell. Quit putting so much effort into the perfect copy, the perfect presentation, all your scripting for your educational training and content, and instead simply learn to…

Entertain or die!

LAW #16

OF THE LEARNIVERSE

"There Can Be Only One"

https://learnistic.com/4116

Yes, this is a reference to Connor MacLeod and the great 80's Highlander movie — a classic if you never watched it — that inspired multiple films and a long running TV series as well.

We have a great myth in society that we should be proud of multitasking because we think it makes us more efficient. People go around bragging about their ability to multi-task as if it were a badge of honor. In reality, it's more like of a badge of shame.

In all my years coaching hundreds of small business owners, the one trait that all struggling owners shared was a *lack of focus.*

It's not even their fault. Society teaches us to multitask, to take on more than we can handle and that doing so is admirable, positioning yourself as the scrambling, hard-working, do it all person everyone wants to be. Don't fall into that trap, doing so is foolhardy and it can tank your business.

My favorite book of all time is "The One Thing," by Gary Keller. This one quote from the book encapsulates the essence of the entire book:

"What is the one thing, such that by doing it, everything else becomes easier or unnecessary?"

Notice the pure clarity of that statement. It doesn't direct you to make a to do list. Instead it asks you to *evaluate your priorities,* to identify the ONE thing that could make the biggest impact on your business, and to focus on just that.

I take this philosophy of "the one thing" to extremes in my business. For example:

- When planning my marketing calendar for the year, I theme it to a single word like "prolific".

- When I create the concept for a product, I force myself to distill it down to its essence as a single word that describes the entire concept. For example, with my mobile learning platform Learnistic™, that one word is "frictionless".

- In my approach to managing tasks via a process I've dubbed as 7-3-1 system, I emphasize selecting the one task that day that can "make everything else easier or unnecessary" and it becomes the first task of the day that I focus on.

- When I focus on my weight loss, something I am continually having to pay a lot of attention to, I go at it in themes, focusing on one approach for a period of time, such as daily walking.

- Even when I set the priorities for my multiple development teams for the week, I theme it around one single feature, so that all are working together towards a single purpose.

In fact, the word "priorities," in the plural form, is an oxymoron. The word "priority" has been around since the early 1400's, but it was always used in its singular form — the word "priorities" wouldn't even exist for another 500 years — it only started being used in the 1940's. This makes complete sense because, how could there be more than one priority? Only one item can be the "most important." But our multi-tasking hyper-busy culture has corrupted the concept of prioritization entirely.

Think about the simplicity of that. Imagine having the clarity of having one *single* priority in your business —the

TROYBROUSSARD.COM LLC © 2020

intense focus on that "one thing" that would make everything else easier.

I have studied and worked with numerous successful entrepreneurs the past decade and I can tell you those that are most successful are intensely focused. Many times their growth spirts come on the back of shutting down various products of divisions of their company — a sort of "forced focus" — that helps them rebound quickly.

You will hear me talk a lot in this book about clarity, focus, "the one thing," and focusing on a single relevant business metric. So, whip out your sword and start taking heads like the Highlander and slash away those other "priorities" because...

There can be only one.

LAW #17

OF THE LEARNIVERSE

"People Are Soap"

https://learnistic.com/4117

Those who have worked with me will tell you, I repeat things a lot. It's a strategy of mine to drill certain fundamental messages and belief structures into your brain through repetition.

(HINT: It's not by accident.)

One of the things I know to be true is that, fundamentally, people are like a bar of soap. Stay with me here because this is important.

When you go to the grocery market and you buy a fresh bar of soap, it has certain qualities.

The bar of soap is rectangular, has a nice, strong scent (at least I hope it does), comes in a box, and can be a bit rough with somewhat sharp edges.

Now, over time, as you use this bar of soap, what happens? The soap begins to evolve. With continued use over time, the bar of soap gets a little less fragrant, its scent a little less potent. It becomes more comfortable in your hand and some of those rough edges begin to smooth out, getting a bit softer as it wears down with the progression of time and use.

But ask yourself this. Did its shape fundamentally change? Did that rectangular bar of soap turn into a pyramid? A circle? An octagon? Does what once smelled like Irish Spring now smell like fresh baked cookies?

Did it fundamentally transform into something it wasn't? Or did it just evolve into a little *less* of what it already was?

My well-cultured belief is that people are no different than that bar of soap. After coaching hundreds of small business owners over the past 15+ years, I can tell you, you too are a bar of soap.

As you age (and I mean that in business years, let's keep it on topic here), you'll likely become a bit more comfortable, refined, and likely even a bit more tolerant. I'm betting that you've probably even smoothed out some of those "rough edges" of your early adulthood.

But you won't fundamentally change.

Sleazy or manipulative salesmen will always find a new mark, a pitch, and product to push. Creators will always keep creating, even if something entirely new or in a completely different manner. Givers keep giving. The kind-hearted won't suddenly turn into tyrants and cranky people will likely stay cranky. And pessimists will continue to see the glass half empty.

So, stop trying to change people and stop trying to change yourself because — surprise! — just like bars of soap, they won't, at least not fundamentally. In time and with great effort you may be able to tame the Lion a bit, but that Lion doesn't transform into a Zebra.

Instead, focus on sorting and filtering people. Are they someone who adds to your life? Or do they take away from it? I don't believe in middle ground — to me, neutral doesn't exist. Even the mailman can scowl at you and foul your mood, or just hand you the mail with a subtle smile and uplift your day, even if just a bit. It's not a bad thing — it's merely accepting people for who they are, and not falling in love with the potential you might think you see. There's even some marriage advice in that line, if you look for it.

Now, to take this further — what if, you could nail down what makes up your "soapiness" — the part of you that is fundamental and that won't change — and embrace it? What if you truly focus on your *one* core strength, refining it with many more iterations of improvement and becoming a true master?

Here's what I mean.

Think of a musician who dabbles with guitar, bass, piano, and the saxophone. They can play all at an above average level and frequently switch between them. Then, compare that musician to the one who does nothing *but* play the sax, night in and night out, playing at every jazz bar that will have him. This musician who focuses on just a single instrument will become far more proficient than the musician dabbling with many. It's simple math. At the end of a year he has hundreds more hours of time focused on just one skill, he can't help but be better.

Most people spend their entire life in a delusional state, lying to themselves, entertaining the notion that they will somehow become something they are not, rather than simply embracing all that they *already are*.

This is true in life as it is business. If you truly understand your business you'll realize it is nothing more than a reflection of you, your values, and your own personal development.

This law of business is simple. But "simple" doesn't necessarily mean *easy*. I dare say, however, this law is the single most important of all. It's so important, that if you learn not a single other thing through this book, I hope you truly embrace this one simple statement:

"KNOW THYSELF!"

Yes, this is simultaneously elementary and simple, yet elusively difficult to achieve. You'll likely spend years in this quest before becoming more self-aware. And as you do, you will evolve and go deeper than you thought. You won't fundamentally change, but the depth of your own self-reflective knowledge and understanding of your own intuition will continually astound you, if you remain on the path of self-awareness.

- *KNOW...* not only what you do well but, even more importantly, what you absolutely *suck* at as well. Remember, the first sign of intelligence is the ability to admit your own ignorance.

- *KNOW...* what you love, what you get fired up about, and what fuels your passion and drive. But also know what drives you abso-friggin-lutely batshit crazy and avoid it at all costs.

- *KNOW...* what inspires and motivates you to stay on path. But, most importantly, in business anyway, is to know your one core strength and focus on going deeper in it, in improving your own mastery.

This may seem obtuse. But it also may be something that you're just not aware of. You may feel that you have many strengths, and I'm sure you do. But, when you really drill into it, these strengths are probably all related to a single core talent. Once you have the clarity of understanding the function that one thing, it is magical and your business will skyrocket.

Know thyself.

It is simple. Powerful. And it is EVERYTHING to your business.

Most choose to live their life in the gray area in between, in the matrix. But what if, instead of trying to change yourself, you simply learned to embrace your own inner strength with full vigor, flaws and all?

- **WHAT IF...** instead of trying to become a lead-generating master, you focused on producing the specific result that is well within your wheelhouse already?

- **WHAT IF...** instead of focusing on the money, you focused on the results you provide for people, their lives, families, employees, and those who they impact? Imagine what the flood of incoming referrals would look like.

- **WHAT IF...** instead of trying to become the next Frank Kern, a good guy by the way, you just fully embraced your *own* strength, your *own* personality, and *your* inner passion?

- **WHAT IF...** you stopped defining yourself by what you don't know, can't do, and need to learn and started defining yourself instead by what you already know, can do, and already excel at?

- **WHAT IF...** you finally, truly realized the all-empowering truth that your income will be determined this year — and in life — not by what you do, but by what you *don't* do? (Think on that for a bit, I dare you!)

- **WHAT IF...** you simply embraced the unique design of your particular "bar of soap"?

When you accept this premise that people are a bar of soap, it's very freeing. It helps you to deal with troublesome clients that just never seem to do things the way you've asked. It helps you realize that the problem lies not within them, but within you for lowering your own standards and allowing them to infiltrate your business and dilute your effectiveness.

It's powerful because you become aware that the flaw is not within them or their approach, but in your desire to try and change everyone that comes to you to become an ideal client, rather than just exclude those that aren't. You can't help everyone and so focus on allowing people to self-select rather than trying to mold everyone into your liking.

Acceptance will bring you far more peace in your business and self-reflective ownership and personal accountability, though tough, will serve you and your business far more than casting blame. If you see the same scenarios repeating themselves over and over again with your interactions with your clients, the painful truth is that you are doing something to create that drama.

Taking responsibility for your own actions rather than casting blame on everyone else, isn't just the adult thing to do, it's the single fastest way to break through the glass ceiling you find yourself trapped beneath.

If you really want to change your business, decide to change your mindset and approach to business. It's not easy. In fact, it's a major shift.

But it is simple.

It starts with knowing yourself and realizing that you, just like your clients, are merely a bar of soap.

LAW #18

OF THE LEARNIVERSE

"Train Your Customers Like You Train Your Dog"

https://learnistic.com/4118

I love dogs, especially Siberian Huskies. I've had four of them over the years, though I don't have a dog anymore and likely won't again for practical reasons. Well, mainly for one reason: I like to travel — a lot. I've been to 27 countries, lived in multiple countries for a sustained period (like 10+ years in Brazil) and even when I'm back in the US, it's hard to keep me contained.

Most people get that homesick feeling and the urge to go home after a while. Me? Nope, not a chance. In fact, after about 45 to 60 days at home, I get "the itch" to get back out on the road again. In my twenties, I travelled around on a motorcycle. In my 40's, I took the whole family on the road in an RV for the better part of a year. Today, as I write this, I just grabbed the family on a whim and a moment's notice, threw them in the big Chevy Suburban and drove to Savannah, Georgia. Why? Because I can, and because I enjoy it.

I'm sitting here, in the pre-dawn hours, in the historic district of Savannah, overlooking the Savannah River, writing, while the family sleeps in. They have their pleasures — I have mine — and I know myself, and writing is one of them.

As much as dogs don't fit into my lifestyle anymore (at least for now), I've trained Huskies for years. In fact, when I lived in Chicago, my Husky, Riley, was so well trained, that when I let him out back to do his business, he would ring the doorbell when he wanted to come back in. He knew the game.

Chicago winters could be brutal. Riley loved playing in the snow — which makes sense as he was a sled dog after all. But since I'm not one, I soon grew tired of standing at the back door waiting for him to decide if he was ready to come in or not. So, I had a doorbell installed on the outside of the house and trained him to use it. I would let him out and when he was ready to come back in, he learned how to let me know.

Riley was also trained on where he could and could not go in the house — and when. For instance, he knew he could sit on the couch in the family room, but was not allowed to go near the couch in the front formal room where my baby grand piano was. In fact, he knew he couldn't even go into that room unless invited. He would walk right down the hall next to it and sit at the edge of the room while I was playing the piano and wait to be invited in. Then, once invited, he'd sprint over and lay down at my feet while I played.

Training a dog, like most things in life, is actually quite easy — it's just that most people are lousy at it because they aren't consistent. Like most things, consistency is all that is required. If I were to ever let Riley up on the couch in the formal front room, he would be totally confused. After all, his entire training was that that room was off limits. That confusion would lead to him not knowing if it was ok now or still forbidden.

Furthermore, it would be absolutely selfish and mean of me to punish him for entering the piano room one day, yet allow it the next. This is what I call emotional training. Though in fairness, that's giving those who practice it far too much credit. I say emotional training because they expect everyone around them to be able to read their mind and their emotional state in order to stay in their good graces. Ever work for someone like that? I say that it's giving them far too much credit because it isn't training at all, it's merely reactionary emotional response.

This is why most people fail miserably at dog training. When they are having a great day they behave one way and with a certain set of expectations of what is acceptable and not from their dog. But the next day, irritated and frustrated by a bad day at work, they treat their dog entirely different and somehow expect him to understand.

To the dog, one day the couch is fine as the owner is feeling down and needs a furry hug. The next, they get scolded for being on the couch. It's a frustrating life for a dog when the owner doesn't know how to train them.

Training a dog is simple, but it requires 100% rigid, firm, disciplined consistency. The same can be said about children. Yes, I know, doting moms will scowl at me at the very notion of training their children like you train a dog, but the concept is absolutely valid and sound. How do I know? Well, I do have four children after all.

My wife frequently asks me why my son jumps up when I ask him to do something but is apparently hard of hearing when she does the same. It's simple. I am 100% consistent with him, and he knows that. I expect the same behavior from him at all times and consistently hold him to that standard. I don't allow him to get away with misbehaving when we have guests but then hold him to a different standard when we don't.

Why am I spending so much time talking about dogs and children? Because training your clients is just as simple and no different.

You can train them to be ideal clients — or you can train them to be over-needy, self-indulging pains in the ass. It's totally your choice. And as in that Rush lyric I mentioned earlier, "If you choose not to decide, you still have made a choice." Think about that for a minute. Either way a decision has been made and either way, you are responsible for it.

How much time have you spent thinking about how you want your clients to interact with you? How much time have you spent creating a training curriculum for them? I don't mean a formal training document that you give them, nor a training program that you send them through. What I mean is a set of internal, specific constraints that you put in place and rigidly adhere to, without emotion, that create a simple, straight and narrow path for their interaction with you.

A dear friend of mine, and business partner in various endeavors, is John Sanpietro. One of the things I most admire about John is his relentless observance of the world of constraints. John is meticulous in enforcing constraints on all he does.

Fridays are reserved for family only. Every Friday, he has a date day with his wife while his son is at school. John won't answer the phone, return an email, view a text, even from me despite being a good friend for more than a decade — nope, not on a Friday.

Likewise, my trusted friend and business partner Ben Settle is not likely to ever answer the phone, even if he sees that it is me calling. He hates phone calls. We may chat sometimes back and forth via the Marco Polo app for a couple of hours on end, but if I were to call him, he would say, "Dude, wtf? Why are you calling me?"

Both have their constraints and they both rigidly enforce them — even with trusted friends and colleagues, so you can guarantee they enforce them with their clients and customers.

A lot of people don't like this train of thought because it implies they are responsible and accountable. Let me be 100% clear and transparent so that there is no confusion on this topic whatsoever. There is no indirect implication intended at all. I am straight up telling you, you *are* responsible for the way your clients interact with you. You and you alone.

- Are you getting too many "needy" clients? You're responsible.

- Are you getting refunds and chargebacks? You're responsible.

- Do your clients frequently miss appointments or show up late? You're responsible.

- Do prospects consistently tell you that they don't have the money for your programs? You're responsible.

- Do you get clients emailing the helpdesk asking about your refund policy? You're responsible.

- Do you seem to attract those with a low commitment to success? You're responsible.

- When something goes wrong, do your clients expect and assume the worst? You are responsible.

I could go on and on, but you get the gist of what I'm saying. While it can suck to have to admit that you're responsible for the situation you're in, there's also a beautiful, albeit painful, clarity in knowing you can create your ideal environment instead. You alone created the situation you're in, and you alone can fix it. There's power in accepting that premise.

You can decide the type of ideal client or customer you wish to work with and set up the appropriate constraints to train them. Or, if you prefer, you can just continue to choose (yes, it is a choice) to live in the matrix of self-imposed victimhood.

But the path is simple: Just train your customers like you train your dog.

LAW #19

OF THE LEARNIVERSE

"Laziness Is To Be Encouraged"

https://learnistic.com/4119

In business, being lazy can be very effective. Well, truth be told, it's not really laziness at all. Those who truly understand the so-called "lazy entrepreneur" realize that they are savants that possess an almost righteous indignation at wasted inefficiency.

Here's what I mean.

There's one group of misfits who are more misunderstood than others and those are the *lazy* ones. While most of society has contempt for the lazy, I have a healthy respect for them because I understand the mindset of *the lazy programmer*.

As you likely know, I'm a *recovering* programmer. I have spent the better part of 25 years programming in various languages. Starting with low level machine language, migrated into graphical interface design, and all the way through object-oriented C++. I also spent a lot of my time in relational database theory, large-scale enterprise software architecture and development, and just about everything in between.

Many managers compare the daunting task of managing programmers to herding cats, and trust me, there's a good reason for that. Programmers are a unique breed. Today, I manage international herds of nomadic cats, all speaking different languages in five different time zones, rest assured the metaphor is definitely not lost on me.

However most managers really misunderstand programming and certainly misunderstand programmers. When it comes to programming, the lazy programmer is to be coveted, not scoffed at. Because the virtues that are traditionally applauded in a society of efficiency and hard work yield a mediocre programmer at best.

Why do I say this?

Let me give you an example. Let's say that I have an algorithm that is sophisticated and complex. This program takes about 20,000 lines of code in order to do its magic. Suppose you apply society's norms to what would constitute a good quality programmer. This person would be diligent, a hard worker, and very efficient in his tasks. If you hired this typical and generally desirable employee you would have a programmer who might find a way to improve that algorithm by 10 or perhaps 15%. They would likely spend *hours* going through the monotonous task of reviewing, revising, and efficiently editing 20,000 lines of code. 10 or 15% is not too shabby as it's still progress, but certainly nothing impressive.

This Japanese Kaizen approach (steady, continuous improvement) has its place, but when it comes to innovative and exceptional programmers, I much prefer *the lazy programmer*. Others may contemptuously scold him as lazy, a procrastinator with a lack of discipline and effectiveness. However, for those who have managed programmers — or if you're like me, having worked with hundreds of them and hired more than a hundred of them myself — it's the lazy programmer who is best for the job.

At first, the lazy programmer will seem like he's ignoring the task at hand and making no progress at all. He may be the man who shows up hours late and blows off work until noon.

But, in reality, he's diligently working on solving it from afar, by taking a step back, letting the problem sink in, and pondering it for a while before sitting down and writing any of the code.

The lazy programmer will spend time just thinking about a problem before he ever sits down to write a single line of code, and he'll do so in the oddest of ways. He may do so while gaming or playing role-playing games till late in the night. But his mind is dwelling on the problem in the background, thinking of a way he can avoid looking at that 20,000 lines of code.

Because he is lazy — he doesn't want to review 20,000 lines of code. He wants something simple, clean, elegant... and something he can code in an hour's time. He does not want to waste an entire day pondering a solution that will take countless hours of code revision.

So, he throws out all 20,000 lines of code.

And the so-called "lazy" programmer sits down and comes up with a solution from scratch.

He knows the inputs and the outputs that he needs to produce. From that set of variables, he sets off to solve the problem in a completely different way. He doesn't want to bother reviewing anyone else's code. He'd rather start from scratch — but he doesn't want to spend three days writing thousands of lines of code. He wants something simpler and easier — because, well, he's lazy. And out of that laziness comes a complete paradigm shift in the approach this programmer takes to solving the problem.

Instead of revisionary, efficiency-based thinking, lazy programmers use innovative, revolutionary problem-solving thinking — from which comes orders of magnitude performance gains. Instead of a mere 10 to 15% improvement, the performance gains of a lazy programmer often are a hundred times those of the efficient programmer: For instance, where an efficient programmer might reduce the load time of an application from 20 seconds to 19 seconds, the lazy programmer may reduce it to one second.

This is all a result of leveraging a completely different mindset. While others condemn and criticize this "lazy" way of thinking, when it comes to development and innovation, I believe that laziness is actually a benefit and creates an atmosphere wherein people can be innovative instead of evolutionary.

The real trick is learning to recognize the lazy programmer in your organization, even if they're not a programmer.

LAW #20
OF THE LEARNIVERSE

"Forgiveness Is Selfish"

https://learnistic.com/4120

If I haven't managed to offend you yet, I probably will with this law.

See, I don't believe in forgiveness. Forgiveness involves a lot of judgment and projection, that you are "holier than thou" and looking down your nose at others as if your forgiveness is something they need or require. I don't believe there's anything to be gained from massaging your own ego and indulging in judging others.

I've learned in my life that very few things are wrong and even fewer right. Most things are simply wrong for you and right for others. Each has their own perspective. Yes, sometimes they may have a warped perspective, but it is still their own perspective, and in their own mind they see themselves as right.

Trying to judge someone from your moral high ground is an egotistical and maniacal waste of time. Instead, I choose merely to <u>accept</u> things. I can't control someone else — hell, I can barely control my own thoughts. So, the act of trying to forgive someone is just a ridiculous notion. Instead, I focus on simply *letting go*, accepting that it is what it is. I relinquish all power that person or situation might have over me and just move on. Yes, I know this goes against every religious doctrine and I'm okay with that.

I know people say "we don't forgive for others, we forgive them for ourselves." Well, isn't that in and of itself a proof of my assertion that forgiveness is selfish? So, if we accept that it's selfish from the beginning, why not practice it as a method that doesn't indulge our own ego or judge others? Why don't we simply acknowledge that forgiveness is for our benefit, and that all we really need to do is just let the person go.

Whether it's a client who wronged you, a chargeback you received, or a lawsuit filed against you, rather than wasting your time pondering whether you should forgive this person, why don't you just move on to running your own life and your own business? Instead of focusing on the person who wronged you, selfishly focus on what's actually important for you and your family. Let go of all drama.

Selfishness gets a bad rap, but selfishness is what drives 98% of our society, whether you like it or not — it's just rebranded and renamed with other more altruistic terms.

But, at our core, we are selfish beings. Our very instincts are derived to protect ourselves and those we love. This is selfishness at its highest form. It's called instinct. Rather than playing the political correctness game, embrace your selfishness and instead focus on what matters — your needs and how you can serve yourself, your business, and your family at the highest level. Doing so might feel selfish, but remember, forgiveness is selfish.

But what about serving others, you ask?

Simple, if you can't learn to serve yourself first and selfishly prosper, how can you possibly serve others? What value can to add to their lives? How can you support them or their philanthropic causes if you're still in the poor house yourself?

Caring for others and serving others comes from a place of balance and confidence, a place that can only be attained by first acknowledging and embracing the simple idiom that forgiveness is selfish.

LAW #21
OF THE LEARNIVERSE

"Be Relentless"

https://learnistic.com/4121

There's very little that can thrust your business forward faster than a relentless tenacity. True relentlessness is instinctual, but it can also be learned. It comes naturally when you have a clarity about your passion. Without clarity, it's hard to have that same drive. And without passion, it's impossible.

When you have an absolute clarity of purpose and focused drive, it becomes that much easier to have a sustained relentlessness that will profoundly thrust your business forward against the competition. When the competition pulls back because of a recession, your relentlessness pushes you forward. When others sit back out of fear, you move forward. You work harder, push harder, relentlessly building your business to be more adaptive and forward-thinking.

My freshman year in high school, I played point guard for the varsity basketball team. This was a small Christian school and we didn't have football, so our homecoming game was a basketball game instead. I was probably the second- or third-best person on the team and usually scored about 15 points a night or thereabouts — hardly a rock star, but competent all the same.

But what set me apart from everybody else on the team was a relentless nature that would never give up. I would show up early to practice and shoot a hundred free throws before anybody else even arrived. And after practice was over, I'd shoot another a hundred free throws. Again, hardly earth-shattering dedication but, as a freshman in high school, it put me above everyone else in my class. It also earned me a starting spot on the varsity squad. For our homecoming game, several of our players were not in the second half of the game because they were involved in homecoming festivities, leaving us with exactly five people for the second half of the game. Me? I refused to participate in homecoming so I could finish out the game.

But it wasn't an ordinary game.

About seven minutes into the first quarter, something happened: I rolled over on my foot as I did a fade-away jump shot and felt something snap. I grimaced — I knew I had broken it. But our team was down by a few points and we were only midway through the first quarter of a game. I knew if I left, because of our reduced team size, it would result in my team playing four against five. And that was not something I was willing to do.

I relentlessly played the entire rest of the game. At halftime, when everybody else went into the locker room, I jogged around the outside of the court because I knew if I stopped moving and let my foot rest, it would swell up and my game would be over.

So I kept moving. Running down the court was painful, and I hobbled at best. My coach scolded me for being a wimp and faking injury.

When he called a timeout, I told him to lay off my ass because my foot was broken, and I was playing through it and didn't appreciate his nagging. He said I was full of crap and that, if it was broken, I wouldn't have been able walk, much less play. I ignored him and kept playing anyway.

At the end of the game, despite my best game of the season, a career high 29 points, we lost by three. We were a huge underdog and should have lost by 20 or more. But by finishing the game, I led an underdog, not to victory, but enduring earned respect from the highly favored league champion.

I did this, not to show off or to prove a point to anyone, but out of a sense of relentless tenacity to achieve the objective. That same inherent relentless tenacity is what allowed me to build multiple seven-figure companies, even after massive losses and complete failures. That tenacity is what allows me to move forward when others retreat.

Relentlessness will serve you well if you can find a way to adapt it into your life and philosophy. So, choose to be relentless.

LAW #22
OF THE LEARNIVERSE

"Consistent Mediocrity Annihilates Bouts of Brilliance"

https://learnistic.com/4122

In a twist on the classic Tortoise and the Hare story, I actually celebrate daily consistent mediocrity. Yes, it seems odd to say that, but here's what I mean:

Consistently making progress daily is the key to growing your business faster than any type of bout brilliance you might have.

Consistency is a sign of hard work — it's something that few have the discipline to master, especially when the improvements seem rather small on a day to day basis. We tend to celebrate the great big victories, the grand slam home runs. But a team that could bunt their way onto base time and time again would defeat any home run king.

While you may have the occasional 20% or even 30% gain here or there, I'll take a slow and steady 1% *daily* improvement over that any day.

In 2019, I lost nearly 90 pounds of weight — a seemingly impressive number, until you look at how mediocre the real progress actually was. While others might lose 20 pounds in two weeks and brag about their success, I was churning along at a mere seven to nine pounds a month in weight loss. However, over the course of that year, the results amounted into something that was transformational. I reached my lowest weight as an adult, my energy levels were through the ceiling, and it was a huge transformation in my physical appearance and health — all based on simple mediocrity.

Each week, I would lose only a mere one or two pounds of weight — which on its face is hardly anything impressive. Yet the transformation that consistency caused was nothing short of miraculous for me. The good news is that mediocrity is not hard to achieve. Anyone who can focus on daily discipline and just moving forward each day in some small area of business can easily leapfrog past those who are much more brilliant but less disciplined.

They say "you should outwork your competition." But success is not about slaving away. It's about making small strides every day without fail.

- It's about going for that daily walk even when it's raining.

- It's about grabbing your boots and trouncing through the snow because you're not going to miss the daily walk that you promised yourself you were going to do.

- It's about discipline.

- It's about consistency.

- It's about focusing on the inputs, not the outputs.

Most of society teaches us to focus on the wins or the outputs, like salary and revenue, and the total pounds lost. But if you train yourself to focus on the discipline of the input side of the equation instead, you'll have far more success. Instead of focusing on how much weight you've lost, instead focus on going to the gym or for a walk every day. Focusing on the inputs is what drives the outputs, because, you can't get the outputs without the work on the input side.

Measure your effectiveness, not on your results attained, but on the work you're putting in. Instead of thinking of the number of sales you made or the amount of revenue you generated, think in terms of the number of lead magnets you created, or the number of leads you generated. These are input-based metrics which will ultimately drive the outputs of your business — fundamentally, you don't control the outputs. You can only control the input.

Focusing on and trying to control the outputs alone is really a silly modern-day definition of insanity, if you ask me. I'll take the daily mediocrity of consistent discipline any day over bouts of brilliance.

LAW #23

OF THE LEARNIVERSE

"Evil Always Prevails,
So Point the Finger"

https://learnistic.com/4123

If you're a fan of comic books or any of the million plus Marvel blockbuster films in the past decade, you should know by now that it's the villain who makes the movie, not the hero.

We all know the hero and all his traits. We like him. We even admire and look up to him. But we go to the movies to see the villain: What will his superpowers be? How hard will the hero's struggle be to overcome him? That's what pulls us in.

One truth that all great moviemakers know is the greater the villain, the greater the box office success. This is a part of human psychology you need to understand if you want to create a powerful brand and business.

In one of my previous SaaS (software as a service) companies, I was up against a much larger company. They had been in business for seven years longer than me. They had all the advantages I didn't. They even had nepotism on their side, as their founder was one of the co-founders of another company we both interacted and did business with.

In short, they were my enemy and I made sure all my clients knew that — they were the villain. People like an "us versus them" storyline. They like to root for the underdog. So, that is exactly the culture I built in my business.

I constantly played the David and Goliath, "poor little us fighting the big dominant player in the market" angle and used it to get more customers, more reviews, more referrals, and more trust and rapport with my clients. By doing that, we shot up from being relative unknowns to the #1 product in our category — even ahead of this "so-called" giant in the industry — all in a record 14-months' time.

Just like I'm not using their name now (though many of my long-following tribe of customers know exactly who I'm referring to), I never used their name then either. In fact, their name was not allowed to be spoken out loud in our company — not in any of our webinars, our calls, our Q&A sessions, or at any other time. I simply referred to them by the villainous sounding "the company that shall remain unnamed."

Do not misunderstand me: I'm not saying this company was bad, evil, or made up of villains. What I am saying is, I crafted a narrative that allowed me to position myself against them and create a culture of "us versus them." We were the underdog which endeared us to our clients in a way that helped us supplant them in the industry in a very short period of time.

This "us versus them" mentality, if properly deployed, is very powerful. It also a weapon you must learn to effectively wield. Some of the greatest companies in the world were built using this weapon — one of the most notable ones being Apple. With its elitist, almost belligerent disdain for Microsoft, Apple created a classic "us versus them" mentality that resulted in the world's first trillion-dollar tech empire. So, yes, I think this strategy might work well for you as well.

People are naturally intrigued by and drawn to controversy and finger-pointing, so give them what they want. You don't have to do it in an insulting way. In fact, I joked and made light of my villain. I had an obvious contempt for them, but I didn't allow it to go to a level of rudeness or unprofessionalism. I did, however, use jokes, thinly veiled parodies, and other clever mechanisms to perpetuate and agitate the "us versus them" mentality, while always tying it back to our empathy for our clients.

Did it work? Hell yes it did. That's how we surpassed them in such a short period of time. This was also evidenced in what happened after I sold the company. Without my leadership (and my leveraging this "us versus them" strategy), my competitor quickly rebounded. That was sad to see — but it was also gratifying to see that they slowly but surely copied most if not all the differentiating features, pricing tactics, and strategies I pioneered.

Had I remained onboard, I know the story would have unfolded differently — but that company was not my long-term vision. Instead, it was one that helped fund my development of Learnistic. That was its purpose — to me — and I don't regret it at all. In fact, it is still a financial asset to me, through a well-structured buyout agreement.

Does evil prevail? No, not really. But it does stoke the fire and it does prevail when it comes to engagement because of the controversy it creates, the struggle with which your clients and customers can identify. In that sense, yes, it always prevails over a wishy-washy, don't hurt anybody's feelings, kinder/gentler, marketing message that has no personality, no soul, and certainly no passion.

As Larry Winget would say, "Grow a pair," and start pointing the finger, and cultivate an "us versus them" climate in your business and leverage it to your advantage.

LAW #24
OF THE LEARNIVERSE

"Preemptively Purge Do-Nothing Do-Gooders Like the Life Sucking Energy Vampires They Are"

https://learnistic.com/4124

Yeah, I know, this sounds a bit over the top but, trust me, this is a matter of self-protection for your business. Do-nothing do-gooders will pompously pronounce their unsolicited advice and so-called wisdom as if it was candy at Halloween, but they do nothing to actually improve the quality of your business. In fact, they do everything to cripple it and detract from it.

In business, you should surround yourself with people who are action takers. Do-nothing do-gooders are exactly the opposite — they run their mouth off about all their opinions, and trust me, they're never short of opinions. But when it comes to taking action and doing something about it, they're the last people to ever show up.

Instead of catering to this low class of society, cultivate a business environment that encourages action takers to be your customers. Those are the people who will get results using what you teach or sell and will become great fans and referral sources for the growth of your business.

The do-nothing do-gooders will simply waste your time like the energy sucking vampires they are. They'll overload your help desk and Q&A sessions with pointless, obtuse discussions that have nothing to do with reality and are all about elevating their own perceived self-importance. They wouldn't know reality if it bit them in the ass, because in order to see reality, they would actually have to do something in the first place. Instead, they just wish to pontificate about the potential impacts of what might happen, and then still do nothing to make that happen either.

Trust me, lose them, expel them, refund them, let them go and move on. Instead of wasting your energy and time on them, focus your time and efforts on those who do take action.

In my group coaching, I have great action taker clients. My most ideal client is Wardee. It's very rare that Wardee misses a call — even though she's a very successful businesswoman with a large list and does not have a lot of time at her disposal. But, every week, she carves out 90 minutes to 120 minutes to show up for our weekly coaching call.

Why? Because she takes action.

What I admire most about Wardee is that she always listens and learns from the advice given by or to others in the group. Instead of tuning out and saying to herself, "this doesn't apply to my business," she does just the opposite. On every call, I can see her thinking, "hmm, I wonder how this applies to my business?"

How else do I know this? Well, when I'm done talking to one of the other group coaching members on the call, she then asks a pertinent and intelligent question relating to the advice I just gave — even if it was about a business completely different from her own. Because not only is she paying attention, but she's looking, and is willing, to learn in her business from others as well.

That alone is quite admirable and a testament to her individual success — but more than that, it is what she does after the call that matters most. Without question, after almost each call, Wardee sends some nugget of information to me in our Slack channel. She tells me what she got from the call and how she's going to try it out. And the next day — yes, I said the very next day — she's already posting results from the action that she took.

This type of client is an ideal client — someone who is willing to learn from others, and capable of taking immediate action. When you surround yourself with clients like this, you absolutely love your business, because every one of them brings an energy to each call that inspires you to further step up your own game. This is one of the reasons why I love curating high quality clients, and why I would much rather have 10 ideal clients than 100 wishy-washy customers who occasionally show up with their video turned off while they're surfing around Facebook in the background and add absolutely zero value.

I don't care about cashing their checks. In fact, I exclude them and refuse to take their money. I prefer to surround myself with the action takers; those are the ones who make business fun. So, preemptively purge do nothing do-gooders like the life-sucking energy vampires they are and watch your business flourish as a result.

LAW #25

OF THE LEARNIVERSE

"Secret Kings Suck"

https://learnistic.com/4125

We all know about the Alpha male — but have you ever heard of the Gamma male? Trust me, this is the type of male employee or client you want to study — and avoid at all costs, to keep them from corrupting and influencing the culture of your business. Gamma males are called "secret kings" because they are a legend in their own delusional self-inflated mind.

Here are their characteristics. They:

- Generally have above average intelligence, but are likely social rejects

- Have difficulty with relationships in particular

- Project their failures on everyone else, refusing to take any accountability for their own miserable coexistence and lackluster effort

- Like to infiltrate organizations and disrupt them, cowardly pointing fingers and causing drama wherever they go, taking pride from showing how smart they are despite no one in the organization wanting to work with them

Gamma males have been multiplying since the invention of the Internet, where they can now cowardly expose their views anonymously without consequence, something they simply wouldn't have the guts to do it in person or in real life.

Behind the protective wall of anonymity of the Internet, they flame people, insult and belittle others while wielding their self-righteous badge of strength: their own cowardly anonymity.

Gamma males are also delusionally dishonest individuals. I say "delusionally" because their dishonesty is so fraught with projection that they begin to believe their own bullshit, so much so they end up lying to themselves as well. In their mind, they can't possibly be at fault for anything (part of their delusion), shifting the blame to everyone else rather than take one morsel of accountability on themselves.

In our businesses together, Ben Settle, and I routinely exclude Gamma males without them even knowing they're being purposefully excluded. We block them just based on their interactions with the help desk from ever purchasing our products.

We prevent them from entering our culture and preemptively strike them down before they infiltrate, demean, and destroy the culture we're creating. I recommend you learn to recognize them, study them, and cast them out of your business and employee ranks as soon as possible. There is nothing is more critical to preserving the quality of your business.

Most Gammas are unattractive and toxic individuals. I don't mean unattractive as in their physical appearance — but the personality they have created for themselves ends up becoming so toxic they tend to repel women and others who meet them by default.

This leads to a self-fulfilling prophecy where they see everyone else as being wrong and that nobody else can possibly understand what they're going through — and by elevating themselves to this "misunderstood" status, they are then known as the Secret Kings.

The Gamma male is a term that was invented by Vox Day. If you want to research these characteristics further, read some of his work. Understanding how to spot them and remove them from your tribe is wise and will protect you from many of their toxic viruses infecting your organization and customer base in the future.

And, remember, Secret Kings suck and need to be eradicated from your business like the cockroaches they are, immediately.

LAW #26

OF THE LEARNIVERSE

"There is only 1MTM
— Know Yours"

https://learnistic.com/4126

Business owners and marketers are fixated on metrics. They will create complex formulas to predict their business growth and try to manipulate future outcomes based upon them. Unfortunately, a lot of it is just mental masturbation. Unless you're a nine-figure business, there is really only one metric that matters, which is why you more than likely should adopt a "1MTM" approach to running your business.

1MTM stands for the "One Metric That Matters".

Now, a lot of people might hear this and think, "Troy, that's ridiculous. How can there only be one metric that's going to determine everything I need to do to run my business?" But that's not the way this works.

The one metric that matters is not about having one metric for the life of your business. Instead, it's about understanding the life cycle, the growth cycle, and the maturity of your business.

Here's what I mean:

There's only one metric right now in your current life cycle. Three months from now, it might be an entirely different metric, but today there's only one that matters. Uncovering it and focusing on it — and it alone — is what drives your business growth with a clarity of focus of a single purpose.

To give an example of 1MTM in a business that most everyone knows, let's talk about Dropbox.

When Dropbox first launched, it was a freemium model. They gave you a free account and allowed you to store some of your files in the cloud for free. If you wanted more storage space, you had to upgrade to a paid account.

In the beginning, the only metric that mattered to Dropbox was, "How many new freemium signups did we get today?"

That's all they cared about. Their entire business was focused around driving this one single metric.

As their business evolved, that metric shifted. If you can recall their growth cycle, you might remember that they started introducing bonuses — additional storage that you could get free if you referred other people. Their strategy and metric evolved, but was still singular in purpose. It was still about driving freemium users, but their new sub metric and their new focus became, "How can we use existing users to drive more referrals?" Their focus shifted from *new freemium users* to *new referrals*. Indeed they had, a new, 1MTM.

Over time, their 1MTM — the one metric that matters — shifted to conversions: "How do we get more of the freemium users to convert into paid subscribers?" Then, as their business model further matured, they again evolved — this time, to a new 1MTM which was all about eliminating churn. In other words, "How do they keep their existing subscribers from leaving their service?"

At each phase of their growth, they shifted and adapted the one metric that matters — but no matter what, they were only focused, with absolute clarity, on that one single purpose within their entire organization.

And that singular focus is what drives viral business growth.

So then, your challenge is to identify that metric. But, before you do that, remember that solving a problem first begins with asking good questions. Look at other models around you that are thriving. Analyze what they seem to be focused on and how that might be applicable to your business.

A good solution always starts with a great question, but there is one undeniable fact: in order to grow your business at light speed with hyper-focused, relentless pursuit, you need to understand and know what that one metric that matters is for you.

LAW #27
OF THE LEARNIVERSE

"Confidence Converts"

https://learnistic.com/4127

People can smell weakness on you over the phone as strongly as any pheromone in the street corner bar. Every great salesperson understands their biggest asset is their confidence.

Every NFL quarterback knows that, after they just throw an interception that's run back for a touchdown, they must immediately shake it off, stand up, and be willing to risk it all on the very next pass. Their confidence cannot waiver. They make mistakes, yes, but their confidence can never be determined by their outcomes.

Ponder that last statement for a minute. Confidence is not shaken by outcomes — confidence is an *input*. If you want to lead others to success in your company or inspire others to follow you in your business, you need to learn how to lead with confidence first.

When you look at traits like leadership, one of the great ways to learn them is through military study. Think of a Marine Corps Lieutenant leading his troops into battle. How likely would the soldiers be to follow him up the hill if he turned back at them, shrugged his shoulders, and asked sheepishly, "Well, should we take the mountain?" Was any soldier ever asked beforehand if they *wanted* to step forward and put their life on the line to charge the hill?

Never.

They were led by someone who inspired confidence and trust and displayed courage under battle.

You may think your business is different, and you may be selling in the health and wellness space and say, "Troy, what does this have to do with battle?" Every business is in a battle, a battle to survive, a battle to thrive against any third-world entrepreneur willing to work three times harder for a third of the money. If you doubt me, that's fine. You'll learn soon enough — and probably the hard way.

Here's another thing about confidence: the level of confidence in those who are most successful borders on arrogance. There's a thin line between confidence and arrogance. The best leaders are those who tiptoe that line frequently with both feet, veering on the side of arrogance.

Am I saying that you need to be an arrogant person to be successful?

Absolutely not.

But I am saying you shouldn't be afraid to be one if that's what's called for. Many of Steve Jobs' closest friends didn't even like his personality that much — but none of them could argue that he was bold, brash, and, yes, confident. And Apple would have never become what it did without him. You don't need to look up to Steve Jobs or even try to become like him, nor even have an aspiration to do so. However, you should aspire to become the strongest version of yourself that you can, because that strong, confident version of yourself is what will lead your business forward. You'll grow leaps and bounds faster than a shy, timid leader will ever inspire, because nothing converts like confidence.

LAW #28
OF THE LEARNIVERSE

"Your Story Has No Competition"

https://learnistic.com/4128

There is only one thing in your business that is completely immune to the competition and incapable of being knocked off. That one thing is *you and your story.*

We all love a good story. Hollywood knows this and pays hundreds of millions of dollars to create and craft the perfect storyline for their movies.

Storytelling has even made its way into business as well in the form of story-based copywriting and even what's called "storyselling." The question is not whether it works but rather, "Are you using it effectively?" Sadly, the answer for nine out of ten businesses is a resounding "no."

If you want to go deep into the world of storytelling, then you need to study the hero's journey. The hero's journey is a framework upon which nearly every single blockbuster film has ever been based upon. While there are a few outliers, most if not almost all movies are based on this framework.

Demystifying the hero's journey is not just a book of its own, but an entire series of books — yes, it's that deep. But the one universal part of the story is the "arc."

The arc occurs as the reluctant hero leaves his dull and boring life and enters an adventure full of challenges (the arc upwards) and then in the end returns to a place of calm, completing the arc.

Officially there are 17 official stages of the hero's journey that really make all of this come to life. I won't go into it here, but I challenge you to spend some time acquainting yourself with this formula for successful storytelling. (It is a well-known concept and just a Google search away.) Then, step up your game, and craft your own hero's journey.

Telling your story in a powerful way is one of the easiest ways to create a culture of inspired followers while completely insulating yourself from your competition — after all, they don't have *your* story. They might have a similar or even a superior product or service, but if they don't have it entangled into a powerful story (which, as I mentioned, they probably don't), you will prevail.

Effective storytelling is something everyone can master — it just takes practice. You don't have to be an epic screenwriter or even a copywriter to learn storytelling.

Effective storytelling is the best way you can possibly sell yourself and your products and services. But it isn't about selling at all — it's a subtle technique that draws your ideal client closely into your fold naturally.

While the 17-stages of the hero's journey is much more elaborate, you can start right now by just focusing on the struggle you had.

Outline your reluctance to embrace the journey you needed to undertake, the discoveries you made along the way, the challenges you overcame and the results of that conquest.

If all of this sounds just a little too "Hollywood" for you, I can assure you it's worth your time. You obviously had a struggle creating your business, your coaching methodology or your software platform. You most certainly learned a few things along the way and I dare say you conquered one or two issues that came up. The fact that you're still in business clearly means that you won that conquest.

That, my friend, is a story — just tell it in your words.

If you follow that short script, you'll be well on your way to crafting a compelling story of your business, product, or service that will allow people to resonate with you and ultimately want to buy from you.

And remember, your story has no competition!

LAW #29
OF THE LEARNIVERSE

"Results are Earned"

https://learnistic.com/4129

Don't fool yourself or buy into the bullshit that has proliferated this industry that some people are just lucky and magically achieved their success. The fact is, every result is *earned.*

Right now, if you're not where you want to be, if you're not making the money you want to make, you must first acknowledge that you're getting exactly what you deserve — *exactly.*

No one gets any more or less than they deserve. Those who are attaining massive results have put massive action into play to attain those results. It may be the result of a single action they took decades ago, or it may be cumulative success accrued through consistent action and time working in their behalf — but the fact remains, results are earned.

I know this will piss off a lot of you because many people like to believe in the lottery mindset — that they're just going to magically inherit success based on how good of a person they are. If you want to buy into that delusion, that's fine. But there are many failed businesses that pave the road to success, that adopted this type of philosophical self-delusion along their meager existence shuffling along their yellow brick road to mediocrity .

I've always been a very hardworking person and I've always outworked everyone I ever knew. It's rare that I ever meet anybody who comes even close to working at the level that I have in my life. Until recently, I wasn't sure that anyone else of my personality type even existed. But when Ben Settle invested in Learnistic, and became my partner, I was immediately impressed by his work ethic. In fact, Ben and I take turns one-upping each other's games, each impressed by the other's devotion. This is a competitive, fun nature that has only served to grow what started out as a friendship into an awesome business partnership.

When we launched the company, Ben, a seven-figure book and newsletter publisher, went back to his freelance copywriting roots by putting me through his secret process for a deep dive into Learnistic, with him as the copywriter and me as the product creator.

It was an arduous process at best and for pragmatic reasons I won't go into it because it is a book in and of itself — in fact, the hours of audio recordings answering his interview questions resulted in pages upon pages of transcriptions that Ben turned into literally hundreds of emails and dozens of hours of audio recordings and trainings for our launch. The fact that he is a great copywriter is true, but the fact that he works harder than any other copywriter I've ever met, even when he hasn't written copy for hire for years, is also very true.

Success is earned. Results are earned. It's more than just about hard work, however. It's about *iterative* work — not striving to master everything under the sun, but instead being content with what you're very good at and being relentlessly consistent and devoted to honing and improving your own core mastery.

The media likes to dilute this truth because they want us to buy into the dream that they're always selling — that magic just happens, and that people become overnight successes or overnight rock stars. The reality is that "overnight" rock star had spent the last 20 years singing gigs four and five times a week at every dive bar he could get to open the door for him before his "big break." There's a reason why he became an "overnight success" — because his success and his results were earned. So are yours.

LAW #30

OF THE LEARNIVERSE

"Nobody Loves a Nuclear Engineer — Lose Your Ego!"

https://learnistic.com/4130

One of the lessons that took me years to learn is, the more successful you are or the more intelligent you are, the more you actually scare people off. I jokingly call this the, "No one loves the nuclear engineer" philosophy. I say that jokingly because I am a former nuclear engineer and submariner in the United States Navy.

For many years, I used to lead with that, from a perspective of trying to impress others. But rather than impressing people or even at least putting them at ease, I would get, "Who does he think he is?" That's the last thing you want to do when you're selling anything or trying to influence people.

Instead, you want to relate to them and allow for them to relate to you. But who can relate to a nuclear engineer? Not many.

You want to bring your message to where they are and not as if you're talking down at them from the need to serve or inflate your own ego either. In general, there's little place for your ego in business. Trying to impress people with how smart you are is probably one of the most destructive habits you can develop. Instead, I like to make light of myself, making self-deprecating jokes to knock myself down a few notches and make myself more relatable and allow people to laugh with me or, even better, *at* me.

I'm perfectly willing to laugh all the way to the bank. A good friend of mine, Tim Johnson, a masterful salesperson, frequently talks about the fact that he'd much rather be wealthy than right. Wise business owners realize the difference, and choose to be wealthy over right every time. They learn to set their ego aside and focus on relating to their clients, at a level which makes them approachable.

But technologists and engineers — or anyone who is a technical or intellectual type — will instead typically focus on being right and, many times, at the expense of pissing off many people around them in the process.

If you suffer from this intellectual affliction, then learn to craft your message as if you were talking to children. Now, I don't mean to talk down at anybody. Instead, explain concepts that are technical and complex in nature, with a level of simplicity, entertainment, and engagement that it takes to captivate the attention of a child, without talking at or down to them. If you can do that, you'll be off to a pretty good start at how to relate with and influence your audience and clients. Children have short attention spans and, trust me, so do buyers.

Focus on breaking down your technology or your presentations, making them easy to understand, relatable, and more emotion-driven, rather than feature and benefit-driven. Learning to craft the message in a way that entertains and engages a child is a cornerstone to selling effectively in today's marketplace. Children can sniff out boredom and will tune out ego-driven narcissists. They will engage but then move on, just as quickly, with complete disinterest. And, as I said, so do your clients.

Most technologists need to work on their charisma and personality. I know that firsthand because I suffered from that for years. If you are a technology geek, don't, you don't have to go off on one of those retreats and strip naked, hugging other men and running thru the forest just to grow a personality. The reality is, you're had it all along. You've just likely thought that it was unprofessional to let it come out. But the irony is, it's actually worse for business if you don't.

Chances are, you're just self-quarantining your own personality and charisma, a recipe that spells doomsday to any business. Instead, fly your freak flag and let that inner personality come out, but do it in a professional and engaging way. Make sure the topics aren't too freaky. I mean, come on. Remember, nobody loves a nuclear engineer.

LAW #31

OF THE LEARNIVERSE

"Yes and..."

https://learnistic.com/4131

A lot of people have problems with saying "no" to their clients and customers in sales conversations. It can lead you to loathe the very business you're trying to be profitable from, wherein you feel enslaved to the very clients you're trying to sell to. It can also lead to regret, anger, frustration, overwhelm, and a general sense of despair in what was supposed to be your solo entrepreneurial gateway to freedom.

I've always been a salesman; it's just something that came naturally for many years. In my thirties, I began studying sales and learned from some of the greats in the industry. Many of the things I was taught were things I was already practicing and just did instinctively without knowing that they were an effective sales tactic. It was just a bit of an instinct for me. And I think that's true for most salespeople.

Yes, they study and refine their art, but I think most salespeople are either naturals or they aren't. Most people aren't very good at sales. In fact, most people's idea of sales comes from a late '80s era used car salesman commercial. That definition is prominent in society. I understand why most people don't like sales.

But, there are techniques that can be taught — especially one simple technique that anybody can apply in their business to pivot a "no" into a potential "yes" — and actually trying to serve your client in a way that helps both you and them, without being argumentative, "salesy," or turning them away.

A lot of times, a customer will ask for something that you simply don't provide in your service. The general answer is to say "no," and that's fine if that's the way you want to be. If you do and it's a hard boundary in your business, I totally admire it.

But there is another alternative you might want to use — it's what I call the "yes and..." technique.

Here's what I mean:

Instead of saying "No, we don't provide printed versions of our training, it's digital only," you could say "Yes, and for an additional $395, I can do that. We sell them in a quantity of three or more. How many do you need?"

Instead of just saying "no" and potentially ending the sales conversation, I'm flipping around a hard no into an opportunity for a sale for an even higher price point than originally planned.

Providing paper copies of one of my products is something I don't normally do — or something I want to do for everyone. So, when I make that offer with the "yes and..." technique, it's generally going to be at a more expensive price point because I am saying, "No, we don't normally do this, but here is what I can do for you."

I'm also giving them the opportunity to spend a lot more money for the yes, if they really want the yes. And, if they do, it's worth it to them, and me. I may have to go out and create this product just for them, so that's why I'm charging more. But now I have given them a path to what they wanted, it's just a question of whether or not they want to pay for it.

What's important when you practice this technique is to make sure you set the "yes and..." price high enough so that if they do say yes, you're not going to be irritated and say, "Oh shoot, now I have to actually fulfill that. I really wished they hadn't bought it." If that's the case, and that's how you feel, then you didn't set the price high enough when you considered your "yes and..." option.

Taking a "yes and…" approach to your business can cater to the affluent on your list who are willing to pay even more money for your product or service if you're willing to give it to them the way they want it. With just one little additional thing added to it, you can deliver a level of personalization and customization that can actually turn into immense profit margins — if you just simply learn to say, "yes and…"

LAW #32

OF THE LEARNIVERSE

"Oh HELL No!"

https://learnistic.com/4132

Of all the lists you're told to make in your business to help you be productive, organized, and everything else, there is really only one list you need to start with. No, it's not your bucket list — it's your "oh hell no" list. This is the list that will define everything for your business.

Your "oh hell no" list should be the first list you make when you go into business and keep building on it as your business grows. As you may have guessed, this list details all of the things that under no circumstance in hell will you allow to occur within your business. Having absolute clarity on what you will not tolerate under any circumstance makes it much easier to define what you will do in your company.

Unfortunately, society has trained us to be politically correct and all worried about dealing with everybody in their own delicate little flower way. Me? I say, "Hell no" to that as well. If you don't stand against something what do you stand for?

I was eating today at a little retro diner here in Savannah, Georgia called Betty Bombers, a hamburger joint that looks like it's straight out of the 1940's. With its World War II era propaganda posters all over the walls, it reminded me of how we used to stand for something. Today, as a society, everybody is afraid to have an opinion they might be criticized for having — and I say "Oh hell no" to that approach as well.

Here's why.

When I looked at the WWII posters on the wall, the one that caught my eye the most was the one of a German soldier in an SS uniform and a big bold statement underneath that said, "This is the enemy." World War II pro-war propaganda is some of the most non-politically correct marketing examples you'll ever find. And, I must tell you, I miss it dearly. Love it or hate it — it at least provoked emotion and thought, and you knew exactly what the message was behind it. This wasn't subtle advertising manipulation — they were outright overt about it.

I'll take somebody with an opinion over somebody who silently tries to manipulate me any day of the week.

Here's a good example:

Once while leading a team in Chicago, I was interviewing for new programmers to add to our staff. During one of these interview, the candidate stood up, slammed his hands on the table, and told me to go fuck myself before storming out the door.

I chuckled in amusement, ran down the hall, tapped him on the shoulder and said, "Hey, where are you going?" He turned around and nearly took a swing at me.

To that I said, "Easy, man — you're hired."

He couldn't believe it. He had told me to go fuck myself... and yet I hired him. But what he didn't know is that the point of the interview was to take him to a breaking point and understand how he would react. And, instead of trying to lie or cover his ass or bullshit me, he had the balls to tell me to go fuck off because he thought I was completely full of shit and out of line. And you know what? I respect that. I respect that person who is willing to stand up for what they believe in, put their opinion on the line, and not care what anybody else thinks about it. They may not be right, and their opinion may not even be constructive for the project at hand, but the fact that they're willing to express it is something that I admire.

So if you want to build your business around the constraints of your life, your morals, and your ethics, then do it — and do it by starting out with an "oh hell no" list.

The very first thing on my "oh hell no" list is wearing a tie. Ever since I left corporate America, I have refused to wear a tie. In fact, I have about a hundred very expensive silk ties, many of them dating all the way back to the '40s and 50's, made from super high-quality Chinese silk — a collection that my grandfather passed down to me. My grandfather passed away in the '90s and I loved him dearly, so I keep them out of deep admiration and love for him. However, I cherish them, but I don't wear them.

Why? Because to me, it represents the noose of corporate America — slowly stifling and strangling the ever-breathing life, creativity, and freedom right out of my body and soul. Can you guess that I hate ties from my ever-so-delicate way of describing them?

The very first item on my "Oh hell no list" is no, I'll never wear a tie again. What's on the top of yours?

LAW #33

OF THE LEARNIVERSE

"A Long-Winded Salesman Snatches Defeat From the Jaws of Victory"

https://learnistic.com/4133

If you've ever studied sales, you've probably spent some time listening to recordings of sales calls. If you're diligent, you've spent hundreds of hours listening to your *own* sales calls. And, if you haven't yet, you should. I can tell you it's a painful journey, but one that will have incredible impact on your ability to close sales.

One thing that I learned from studying sales early on is: there's nothing potential buyers love more than the sound of *their* own voice. The less *you* try to talk somebody into a sale, and the more you let them talk *themselves* into a sale, the better off you'll be. But most inexperienced salesmen do just the opposite.

Mathematically, you can predict the outcome of a sale just by the percentage of time that you're talking versus the percentage of time that the prospect is talking. The more you hit the mute button, the more your checkbook will grow. Instead of running off your mouth off with verbal diarrhea, learn that the mute button is your friend.

Ask piercing, specific questions that demonstrate your expertise and illustrate their incompetence — and then be silent. Allow your prospect to answer them. Sometimes, a long, painful silence in the process can be the most powerful form of sales you can practice.

Questions should be framed on getting to the heart of the matter — not about your product, but about their *why*, about their *need*, and about the *emotional reason* behind their purchase. The more you can help them get clarity through probing questions, the more you allow them to talk themselves into the sale.

Successful salesmen know that it's not about browbeating their prospects with features and benefits of your products and service. Instead, listen intently to *what* they're saying — and *how*. Analyze their voice and speech patterns, internally reflecting on their style, pace, and cadence and reflecting it back to them in a similar style that resonates with them. But, mostly, shut the hell up and listening intently to their needs and desires, not your own.

Ironically, in exit interviews that I've conducted with successfully closed customers, both for myself and for clients who I've coached in the past, the one thing they all had in common was, "Wow, he was such a good salesman and listener."

By saying that, they really mean that they love the sound of their own voice, as do we all. But the more you allow them to talk about their problems, the more they'll trust you — and the more they'll look up to you as someone who provides wise counsel and guidance.

However, when you run off at the mouth, they'll run for the hills. Remember to not be that long-winded salesman who *snatches defeat from the jaws of victory!*

LAW #34

OF THE LEARNIVERSE

"Boldly Claim Your Niche"

https://learnistic.com/4134

Other than your mom, there's probably no greater fan of your own work than yourself. If you're not willing to go out and stake a claim on your own capabilities and your business, then who else will?

I'm not saying to exaggerate and make claims you can't substantiate. That's certainly a recipe for disaster and an outright lie that I would never encourage. But, when you have the goods, you must let people know it if you expect them to do business with you — and claiming your niche is the best way to do it. Proclaiming your confidence and leadership within that niche will inspire others to follow suit, join your list, check out your products and your services, and eventually become customers.

People want to follow leaders and leaders boldly claim what is theirs. They don't wait to be appointed to the task by someone else.

There are many ways you can do this, all depending on your preferred media and format. You can do it by launching a podcast in your niche and growing a devoted audience or writing a bestselling book and representing and positioning yourself well.

I've effectively done both of the above and both were instrumental in my business growth. There are of course a million and one different platforms you can use, so the media should not be your concern. What should be is your attitude and how you demonstrate that leadership.

The easiest way to do that is with products and services that demonstrate your aptitude. It's one thing to boldly claim your niche but it's another entirely thing to demonstratively claim it through leadership, offers, and sales.

If you're going to proclaim yourself as the leader in your niche, you need to lead. That means you need to outdo the competition in terms of quality, polish, and coming across in a different way that positions you well and uniquely.

You don't always necessarily need to be better, but you certainly need to be different. That difference has to be something you can celebrate and confidently lead with.

Many years ago, in the Infusionsoft space, I did this by launching an international bestselling book entitled, *Infusionsoft Mastery*. The title alone proclaimed my mastery of the niche. But, more importantly, the book was well-received and became the leading publication in the industry. My readers would literally quote my book at the Infusionsoft annual conference when asking questions to the CEO.

It was quite a thing to witness, sitting there in the audience and hearing somebody stand up and say to the CEO, "According to Mr. Broussard in his *Infusionsoft Mastery* book..." and ask their question.

That is what claiming a niche is all about — positioning yourself so strongly in your corner of the industry that you cannot be ignored, and boldly leading when others stand back in the shadows.

This one book led to hundreds of thousands in revenue for me over the last few years in referrals, references, customers, coaching and mastermind sales, and other doors that were opened because of it — all because I stepped up to claim my mastery and claim my niche. I encourage you to find a way you can do the same.

LAW #35

OF THE LEARNIVERSE

"Proof Can't Be Unseen"

https://learnistic.com/4135

One of the reasons infomercials can be so successful, especially the QVC-style infomercial, is they're all based on demonstrable proof. They make some miraculous claim and then, much to your amazement, they show you as it happens right in front of your face. You can't help but then jump on the bandwagon and snap up one of those magic cleaners before they all disappear.

Like it or not, proof cannot be unseen. This is important in the process of "subtle selling" within your business.

Subtle selling is selling through demonstration and positioning — and creating a sales process that has nothing to do with sales. Instead, your sales process should show and drip bits of information that makes somebody aspire to do business with you. Storytelling is a great example of subtle selling, but another great method of subtle selling is using powerful proof that your business products and services work.

Client case studies, charts, graphs, and images that show results, results, and more results. The more you can show proof your business is getting what it promises for your customers, the easier it'll be to obtain new customers.

Now, you don't want to overdo this. Remember, the focus is on subtle selling. You want this to be dripped in and weaved into your storytelling, marketing, and emails in a nonchalant and subtle way. This is not an in-your-face sales attempt, but rather just a casual mention. The interested person then looks deeper into your content based on your casual reference as it teased them into wanting to know more.

When you try to pitch hard and pour on the proof, you trigger your prospect's bullshit radar. It will immediately go off and say, "Wow, this guy is trying hard. Something doesn't feel right." But, when you just make a casual reference or show a quick chart or celebrate a client victory (i.e., celebrate someone else's success instead of your own), it has much more power.

When speaking from the stage, I used to always leave all the social proof in the slide deck for my presentation — but I didn't include it in my actual talk. You've surly seen presentations where the speaker talks up all the great things he's done, all the great people he's helped, and all the tremendous results he's provided and blah blah blah boring blah, for several minutes on end. The problem is, all these types of presentations feel the same. This approach can create a negative response instead of a positive one because it feels like you're trying too hard.

So, instead, I leave all that content up on the screen. But, in a self-deprecating way, I would just click past those slides and say, "You know, you guys didn't come here to hear about 17 businesses I started, and how many thousands of clients I've helped," and go then go straight to the meat of the presentation. I do that purposefully. I could easily delete those slides — and many people would naively go too far and edit their presentation that way.

But instead I choose to subtly sell and position myself by allowing that content to be there and allowing them to see it… but in a confident, looking out for them approach, I go through it quickly and show I am trying to do them a favor by not torturing them with all the details. That type of casual approach will go well with your audience because they won't feel like they're being sold to. Instead, they'll feel like you're casual, don't take yourself too seriously, and that you're looking out for their best interests in an entertaining way.

These are subtle selling techniques that work well when you master them, but it's all based on the same principle — and that is, "proof cannot be unseen". Even though I skipped through the slides quickly, they couldn't help but see the world map slide that had little pins everywhere I had traveled in the last year. I skipped through it quickly, but they couldn't unsee it — and the impression it made is that, rather than bragging about it, it was so normal for me that I didn't have to give it the time of day.

That amps up the confidence factor, and it certainly makes you more relatable, approachable, and creates more trust and rapport with the audience than just standing there like a used car salesman telling them how important you are, beating your chest. Equally so, however, I didn't delete the slides.

Find ways in your business where you can casually introduce more proof, without having to drill it into your client's heads. Instead, merely make subtle references and inclusions in your emails, books, webinars, and presentations from stage. Even if you gloss over them, make sure they're there so your clients see them, and it resonates with the positioning you're creating.

Why?

Because proof cannot be unseen.

LAW #36

OF THE LEARNIVERSE

"It's Not Bragging If Your Case Study Says It"

https://learnistic.com/4136

My first car was a 1967 Camaro convertible. My father and I bought it together when I was 12 years old with the intention of fixing it up, to be my first car when I became old enough to drive. It needed some work and it was meant to be a father-son project.

I asked him about how I would keep my friends from pressuring me into letting them drive it as everybody loved muscle cars, especially convertible Camaros, and I didn't want one of my friends to wrap it around a California Redwood tree. At the time, my sister had a 1964 Chevrolet Impala Super Sport and I knew she had dealt with similar issues so I was curious what my dad would suggest.

He responded with a wise lesson that I still use today in many forms. He told me I just needed to blame him, a neutral third party, so I didn't have to look weak in front of my friends, nor have to argue with them or lose any friendships over it — I could just simply make him out to be the bad guy.

He told me I could say, "My old man helped me build this car and buy it and there's no way in hell he's going to allow me to let anybody else drive it. He said he'd take my insurance and keys away if I do."

He gave me permission to make him the bad guy so I could save face. I thought that was a very clever strategy, one I used in many ways later in life.

Ultimately, the father-son restoration project was never completed and I never did get to drive my '67 convertible. But I did benefit from it, by selling it and using the funds for a down payment on my first house — so it certainly served its purpose, though not in the way it was intended.

The point is you can use a neutral third party to either bolster your position (such as, setting boundaries) or, as I will explain, to sing your praises for you, in a way that allows you to sell yourself, your business and your products without having to stand out there pounding your chest and coming across as an arrogant salesman.

Traditionally, people do this via testimonials — but there's a better, subtler, and more powerful and effective way. It does take a little bit of extra work, but the rewards you can reap are well worth the extra work and cost.

Testimonials are good and they have their place, but they can sometimes feel a little bit contrived. They can even leave prospects questioning why this person gave the testimonial in the first place. Even if you stipulate that it was unsolicited and that no incentive was given, there's always a seed of doubt — which is why their effectiveness can be somewhat tainted.

A more creative and powerful way to accomplish the same thing is through customer case studies and interviews. A testimonial is ineffective when the person doesn't do a good enough job of singing your praises — they can either sound over-exaggerated (which then brings the above objection to mind) or, worse, be nonspecific and not say much of anything useful at all. This is why a case study interview, where you can direct the conversation, can be even more effective than an overly effusive or too generic testimonials.

By directing the questions, you can coax out some of the pain points behind *why* this person chose to work with you, what their situation was beforehand, and the full transition they made afterwards by working with you.

It does take some practice to do this effectively, and you must spend some time scripting your questions in such a way that it doesn't sound even worse than a testimonial. Because, at the end of the day, these case studies are not just about them singing your praises. They are opportunities for your customers to connect to *their* story and *their* struggle — and see themselves in *their* shoes as people who also can benefit from your services or products.

A casual interview with previous happy customers, talking about their situation and their business and where they were at — and how much they improved since — will allow your potential customers to connect and resonate with them and their story.

It draws them in and makes them feel optimistic that they can make the same progress too. Even better is if you provide a PDF summary of the case study. It could have the full transcription if you like, but that's not necessary.

You can also create a short booklet that lays out the highlights of the case study with charts and graphs and any supporting data that you can show. Consider this like a college presentation, documenting the success of your specific methodology and offer. It should feel revealing and transparent, and the more data and charts you can show, the better.

Interview quality will also make a big impact here. When possible, have a film crew do the interview. Make sure they get a couple of different angles when they're filming, especially a slight side angle — vary it up so they're not just staring straight down at the camera or the interviewee, as that can have an intimidating look.

If you really want to understand how to replicate this look, watch the show *60 Minutes* or any documentary film and you'll see how they typically position the camera slightly off-center.

It doesn't have to be expensive to hire a professional to do this, as you can find many people who have the equipment and are willing to do it on services like Craigslist and other local community forums. I've hired many people to do this for just a couple hundred dollars. And, in some areas, you might be able to find people willing to do this for free in order to build their portfolio.

Audio and video sound quality also make a big difference. Make sure whoever does this has the proper equipment to get high-quality sound and make it a professional result. Using a professional crew also helps with subtle selling as they are a neutral third party — which is much more powerful than you jumping up and down beating your chest, browbeating your prospects into submission.

One powerful filming technique, and you'll need to specify this to your film crew, is to use a wide open aperture to create a nice blurred background effect. This softens the look, is more natural and resonates more with people because this is how our eye naturally sees imagery — the things we are looking at are in focus, those in the peripheral blurred.

This cinematic look is not hard to create with a DSLR camera, but it can't be done with an iPhone, so make sure your crew has the right equipment. This approach will dramatically up your quality game and impress viewers with the cinematic film style (and it's just not that hard or costly to do).

Just think about what your reaction would be to a shaky iPhone case study video with sound cutting in and out, versus watching a beautifully produced cinematic short film with crystal clear audio. Now here's the ironic thing about this. You've done it right if they don't notice. If they don't notice then it means that there were no odd skips, sound cutting out, focus issues, etc... nothing for them to be distracted by and they're just drawn into your story telling. THAT is what you want.

Subtle selling tactics like this are powerful, especially combined with storytelling. And remember, it's not bragging if your case study says it.

LAW #37

"Learn Your ABC's"

https://learnistic.com/4137

No, I'm not going to talking about the ABC of sales (Always Be Closing). That slogan you've likely heard hundreds of times, and probably most from network marketing or MLM companies. It has been overused to the point of ridiculous.

There is a lot of truth in it, however. Wise salesmen know how to subtly practice it. But this is not about sales — this is about what leads your business forward.

Notice I use the word "lead." That is critical, as I've talked about it in many of these Laws of the Learniverse.

This ABC I'm talking about stands for "Always Be Charismatic."

Charisma is the one thing that most inspires leadership. Charisma is one of those words that encompasses a whole subset of traits and characteristics. It's what makes it so powerful. You always hear of a charismatic leader, because the two go hand in hand. Leadership is fostered through charisma, and charisma inspires leadership. Charisma *fuels* leadership.

Charisma also encompasses confidence. Look at somebody who is charismatic, and you're not going to find somebody sulking in the corner. They're the person up in front, leading by example and attracting those around them to pay attention.

One of the most charismatic leaders of our times, love him or hate him, was Steve Jobs. I know Windows aficionados are going to say Bill Gates was his equal. From a purely financial perspective, that argument may be true, or at least very close. However, Steve Jobs knew how to be a leader — a charismatic enigma who inspired people to put their faith in him and to follow him.

Bill Gates, on the other hand, couldn't lead himself out of a paper bag. I always imagine meeting Bill Gates and shaking his hand, and feeling a limp wrist, wimpy shake that would send me, like Det. Adrian Monk, reaching for a wipe afterwards. The man is undoubtedly very intelligent and has crafted a huge industry around Microsoft Windows. I have enormous respect for him. However, nothing about the man is charismatic.

Charisma is what gets people to follow you, to come in on the weekends to work on that project the business critically needs — not because they have to, but because they believe in your vision, they believe in *you!* Charisma is something that is hard to define, but you can foster it, study it and become more effective at it.

It all starts with leading, and focusing on, charisma in everything you do. When you create videos, let your charisma flow. When you create audios, don't sound like a robot. Let some passion exude from your voice. When you write, have the audacity to express an opinion that exudes leadership and inspires those who read to follow you. And when in doubt, remember the ABCs of business… always be charismatic.

LAW #38
OF THE LEARNIVERSE

"Unapplied Knowledge Is Worthless"

https://learnistic.com/4138

Today, many people as entrepreneurs engage in a practice called "knowledge accumulation." They suffer from squirrel syndrome, buying the latest and greatest shiny object as fast as they come across it. Each time they purchase another course or training, they take one step closer to becoming a digital hoarder — no different from people on those nasty TV shows who cannot even walk through their own house for all the piles of crap they have laying around everywhere.

Digital hoarders are even worse because they waste a much greater resource than space — they waste time. It's not even about the money they waste — it's just about the time.

Why?

Money can be replaced, time cannot. There's a tremendous opportunity cost in chasing every bright, shiny object you come across. And the cost is opportunity lost in the form of the time you've wasted.

Now, you may take a contrarian approach to my statement and say, "Well, Troy, if they didn't actually do anything with the content anyway, then what time did they really lose?" Well, it's worse than that.

Here's how:

- The few minutes spent purchasing the product was completely wasted. But, realistically, it was more than just a few minutes because;

- A person who digitally hoards is someone who has gone back to that sales page numerous times, trying to talk themselves into why they should or shouldn't buy it. And;

- When purchasing, they've already convinced themselves that "this time is going to be different." After just "one more good look," they've decided to make that purchase because because, this time around, they will *really* go through with it.

As my friend Ben Settle would say, in reality they're just *paying* for it. This means that they're not actually *investing* their time — they're simply *spending* money, and that is also a waste. If you don't treat money properly, how can you ever expect it to do right by you?

Also, knowledge in and of itself is absolutely useless. It provides no impact in your life or the life of others. It's only useful when you act and try to apply that knowledge. Notice I said "try "— because, the truth of the matter is, it is going to take many attempts, maybe even hundreds of attempts to apply that knowledge before you find your own unique way to do it and be successful at it. But that is where the magic happens, where you have the intersection of action and knowledge, not merely the digital hoarding of information.

If you suffer from this tendency of digital hoarding, — of accumulating but never really consuming — then I challenge you to not buy another single thing for the next *three months*. Instead, go back and look at one of the recent purchases you've made that you feel could be impactful. And go through it not once, but *three* times.

When you go through your training of choice three times, you'll go deeper with each level of repetitive learning and exploration. And that repetitive process will yield 10x the results than if you were to go through it just once casually without paying attention, as most people do. You'll see these people pat themselves on the back that they made such a valiant attempt at studying and learning. You'll also see them brag on social media about how many books they've read or courses they bought. But, in reality, they haven't put a damn thing into practice from any one of those purchases.

Instead of following the herd and going wide and bragging about your digital hoarding and knowledge, why not try something different and go deep, and practice what you learned? Put it into practice, reap the rewards and turn those purchases into actual business *investments* instead. Remember, unapplied knowledge is worthless.

LAW #39

OF THE LEARNIVERSE

"Laugh at Yourself First and They'll Follow"

https://learnistic.com/4139

I first started speaking from the stage when I was 16 years old, giving a talk in a foreign language that I had learned just 90 days prior, in front of a crowd of over 2000 Brazilians in the São Paulo International Rotary Convention.

In the 30 years since, one of the things I have learned is to disarm the crowd with self-deprecating humor. Being able to point out your own flaws, lower your ego, and have fun and laugh at yourself, really disarms people and a crowd in general. Allow them to join in the fun and see that you don't take yourself too seriously. Maybe they'll even laugh a little with you or at you — hey, whatever it takes.

Regardless, it is a powerful way of breaking down some of the awkward tension that naturally occurs when you are on stage in front of people. The same humor can be used in any form of marketing, whether it's speaking from stage, writing, creating audios, podcasting, creating a video log or marketing on YouTube.

It doesn't matter what the medium is, the principle is still the same. Being able to laugh at yourself and show others that you don't have a fragile ego, inspires trust and confidence in them that you are a leader who's strong enough to be able to laugh at him- or herself. Laughter is great for business in any form.

Remember, people want to be entertained. It's hard to think of calling someone entertaining, without thinking of how they made you laugh. Being able to laugh is one of the principal forms of entertainment. It's one of the most effective ways you can disarm people and allow them to open up to you and what you're selling.

There is a real subtle but powerful air of confidence you exude from being able to laugh and joke with people, to put them at ease, and make them feel good in your presence.

Ultimately, your job in business is to lead your tribe. To do that, you need to inspire them and entertain them. Laughter is a big part of that. Having a sense of humor is a tremendous asset to your business. Going back to the Steve Jobs versus Bill Gates analogy, Steve Jobs would occasionally tell jokes on stage or mock things that went wrong in the middle of his presentations, laughing at himself and allowing the crowd to laugh with him.

In comparison, Bill Gates always seems like he needs to grow a personality and generally shies away from the stage. I can't think of one real meaningful or profound speech that Bill Gates has ever given — though I'm sure he's given many.

But, contrast that with Steve Jobs, who had an entire litany of profound speaking engagements, many of which have gone viral and still resurface on social media from time to time. Most of them involved a degree of not only showmanship, but entertainment and laughter, along with whatever teaching lesson or promotion he was giving.

So, don't take yourself too seriously. Learn to open up a little bit, especially if you make a mistake or blunder, rather than trying to move on and pretend it didn't happen. Poke fun at yourself. Make light of it and allow those around you to joke with you, have fun, and release a new energy and charisma into your followers.

Remember, laugh at yourself first and they'll follow.

LAW #40

"Iteration Trumps Perfectionism"

https://learnistic.com/4140

We all know, or at least should be aware of, the utter ridiculousness of pursuing perfectionism as a life or character trait — especially when it comes to running your business. But what is less obvious is how perfectionism impedes progress through the lack of iteration.

Here's what I mean:

When you focus on a project from the mindset of perfectionism, the project goes uncompleted, or at least is delayed significantly, sometimes for months.

The perfectionist mindset wants to relentlessly and meticulously perfect every single iota of the project, even if to the project's detriment. However, when someone doesn't share this mental defect of perfectionism, they tend to create — and complete — projects that may be almost haphazard in nature in their very first go at it.

Because they're able to get over themselves, do what they need to do to complete it, and move on, they're able to create many more iterations of that same project, refining it quickly, learning and adapting as they go. In essence, they make far more progress and better improvements through *doing* than a so-called "perfectionist" ever could through their process of *projection*.

See a pragmatic realist doesn't have this defective perfectionist gene in his DNA, so he just *does* and *completes*. In the doing, he learns, refines and improves. A perfectionist, however, isn't doing anything at all, they're just *projecting* what they suppose *might* occur. So the irony here is that in the iterations of refinement the pragmatist will outperform the perfectionist every single time.

Here's what I mean about this discussion of iteration. Consider that you're creating your master class for your particular methodology. A perfectionist will take many months trying to get everything just perfect. But instead if you focus on getting it done first and then making improvements, you'll allow yourself to get into the sales quickly, make cash flow and pay for numerous improvements and iterations as you go. You'll more than likely make several refinements to your course and many sales before the perfectionist even completes the rough draft.

More importantly these iterations and refinement are based on actual sales and customer feedback. A perfectionist merely sits around mentally masturbating and pontificating about the potential and never really allows it to become reality. Perfectionists solve nonexistent problems and waste enormous amounts of time doing so.

Iteration is essential in the entrepreneurial world when our clients' needs are often not aligned with what we think they should be. The perfectionist spends months creating the perfect program that nobody ends up wanting. Meanwhile, the pragmatic realist quickly slams out a first iteration to see if it has some impact — and, learning from it, if any pivots or adjustments are needed, releasing the second iteration, learning from that release, then quickly releasing a third, fourth, and fifth, and so on.

And, the next thing you know, in the same amount of time that the perfectionist may have completed his one abysmal failure of a project, the pragmatic realist has released eight to ten revisionary improvements on their already completed albeit provisionary project, and made some money too.

In Australia I was once sternly reminded of the decrepit fallacy of perfectionism by none other than Tony Robbins himself as he stared me down from three feet away. While attending one of his events, he turned and looked me straight in the eye, pointed a gigantic incriminating finger in my face and said, "Remember perfectionism is the lowest form of human development."

That extended arm and pointing finger of his felt like a six-foot long sword piercing into my skull as it revealed my inner delusions with perfectionism.

That moment is something that will stick with me forever — partly because Tony Robbins is a friggin' giant who looks to be about nine feet tall and has a head the size of a small VW Bug, so when the guy stares you down and points at you, calling you out publicly in front of thousands, it kind of commands your attention.

But more than that, I'll never forget it because of the painful clarity that it thrust into my life. I grew up with a perfectionist father. Letting go of perfectionism has been a labored peeling of the onion process I've engaged in for my entire life.

So, hearing somebody so respected in the industry absolutely trash the concept of perfectionism was a profound moment for me. He went on to back up his assertion by saying, "We all know perfectionism is absolutely 100% unattainable, and so the pursuit of it is the very definition of insanity and stupidity."

And yeah, he kind of yelled it at me.

When you think of it like that, it makes a lot of sense. And, over time, I've realized that perfectionism really stems from fear— fear of releasing that product, fear of trying to sell that course, fear of not being good enough, fear of failure. So rather than going ahead and just doing what it is you have to do, instead, you use "perfectionism" as a way to procrastinate and never have to face your fears.

Perfectionism is also a sign of the ego — and an overinflated one at that. Why? Because the thinking that you alone know what perfection is, is in and of itself completely ridiculous and borderline delusional. So instead of embracing perfectionism as a character trait, redefine it in your mind as the very definition of insanity and stupidity — and learn to focus on iterations instead.

LAW #41

OF THE LEARNIVERSE

"Stop Raking Leaves"

https://learnistic.com/4141

Sometimes you can learn much more in life by learning what *not* to do than what *to* do. Growing up, my family was lower-middle class. I wasn't poor and we never wanted for food, but we never had two spare nickels to rub together.

In my entire childhood, we only took one family vacation, which was a disaster rivaling that of National Lampoon's vacation. We drove up at a place that had all these beautiful brochures, only to find out it was a parking lot with tents on gravel and had virtually gone out of business three years before. Ironically the place was called "U Wanna Kamp." Camp was spelled with a "k" and trust me, you didn't wanna.

As a young child and even teenager growing up, I was often puzzled by some of my dad's habits. We lived on about five acres of property with lots of trees and, in the evenings and nearly every weekend, I watched my dad, now deceased, spend the entire day raking away every leaf from the ground.

I was baffled by this concept because, as he would rake, I would watch the wind blow, making leaves fall right on top of the areas he had just raked. Then, he would go back and redo that area too. I could write a whole book from the lessons I learned about my dad and his leaf raking adventures. But the most profound lesson I got was that was I did *not* want to model his behavior.

Later in life, as I matured, I reflected back on my dad's leaf raking. I realized raking leaves helped my father escape from the doldrums of his life, a never ending financial disappoint in his own eyes. He provided for us, kept us safe, fed, clothed — we never wanted for food or shelter. But it was always abundantly clear by the look on his face that he was disappointed in himself and how life had turned out for him.

By keeping a spotless yard, even if it lasted for less than a day, he felt like he was accomplishing something. He could *see* the fruits of his labor, it was tangible. But it was a grand illusion, because what he accomplished had no real bearing on the quality of life he was providing for any of us. Yet, in some masochistic way it made him feel better, seeing that what once was a ground full of leaves was now cleaned up, at least until the winds came again the next day.

As he got older, the same was true with his vegging out in front of the TV. I never understood, as a teenager and later young man, why he wasn't trying harder to make *something* when we didn't have much of *anything*. Instead, he used TV to numb his pain and self-medicate.

Unfortunately, I've seen these same patterns repeat themselves in many small entrepreneurs' businesses as well. They get lost *raking the leaves* in their business doing all the little tedious, monotonous and mind-numbing busy work that has no real bearing on the outcome of their business.

These activities certainly don't do anything to contribute to the bottom line — and if anything, they detract from it. But somehow, they perceive they're receiving some benefit or affirmation from this.

This behavior usually stems from a fear of doing the one thing they're most afraid to do. They don't take action and do the work that they truly need to do — i.e., the real work that will put zeros in their bank account. Rather, they convince themselves that those other tasks are more important, such as:

- Creating yet another funnel that will never be built out or fully deployed

- Editing the next video series three times over only to throw it out entirely in disgust a month later

- Continually focusing on writing just a few more words in their book, which has been a work in progress for the last six years and isn't even relevant anymore

To reference a great song from the '80s band Styx, one of my favorites, they're just *"Fooling themselves"*.

By raking their digital leaves instead of doing actual productive work in their business, they are almost guaranteeing failure — which is ironic considering that is the result they fear the most. This is the irony of irrational fear in general. Fear keeps us from doing the things we know we need to do, and makes achievement almost impossible, this then creates the self-fulfilling prophecy as we, in the non doing, ironically get exactly what we've most feared all along, failure. Our fear itself has guaranteed our failure.

What digital leaves are you raking in your business today?

And don't fall into that BS myth of outsourcing for the raking of those digital leaves either. What's the point in paying three dollars an hour to have the digital leaves raked when in reality you just need to stop raking them entirely? That's even more delusional. There are so many things in your business that are completely unproductive and a complete waste of time. Outsourcing is not the solution, *eliminating* is.

So, before you outsource another task, ask yourself why you're doing it in the first place and if it's really needed. Because you should try three times as hard to eliminate mundane, tedious work as you do to outsource it. Turn off the TV, get off Netflix, start building your business, and stop raking the damn leaves!

Disclosures and Disclaimers

All trademarks and service marks are the properties of their respective owners. All references to these properties are made solely for editorial purposes. Except for marks actually owned by the Author or the Publisher or where otherwise expressly indicated, no commercial claims are made to their use, and neither the Author nor the Publisher is affiliated with such marks in any way.

Unless otherwise expressly indicated, none of the individuals or business entities mentioned have endorsed the contents of this book.

<u>Limits of Liability and Disclaimers of Warranties</u>

This book is a general educational information product and is written for adults eighteen years old or older. Children below the age of 18 are not permitted to consume this content, even if authorized by a parent or guardian.

This book and the content provided herein do not take the place of legal, financial, tax, physical, or mental health advice, or any other advice whatsoever from your attorney, financial advisor, medical professional or other professionals.

Every effort has been made to ensure that the content provided is accurate and helpful for our readers at publishing time. However, the content is not an exhaustive treatment of the subjects. No liability is assumed for losses or damages due to the information provided, including all references to products and services created and maintained by other individuals and organizations. Any representations made about these products and services reflect the Author's honest opinion based upon the facts known to the Author at the time this book was published.

The materials and content in this book are provided "as is" and without warranties of any kind either express or implied.

Printed in Great Britain
by Amazon